Kinship & Imagined COMMUNITIES

Renée M. Bonzani

Kendall Hunt
publishing company

Cover image © Shutterstock, Inc.

Kendall Hunt
publishing company

www.kendallhunt.com
Send all inquiries to:
4050 Westmark Drive
Dubuque, IA 52004-1840

ISBN: 978-1-5249-9151-7

Published in the United States of America

Dedication

To my children, Isabel and Marcel, my Living Assistants in China, Xiaoxi and Seven, my students, and my mother and father, Rogene and James, and Roger, Jimmy, Lori, and Linda, friends and family, for all their help.

Table of Contents

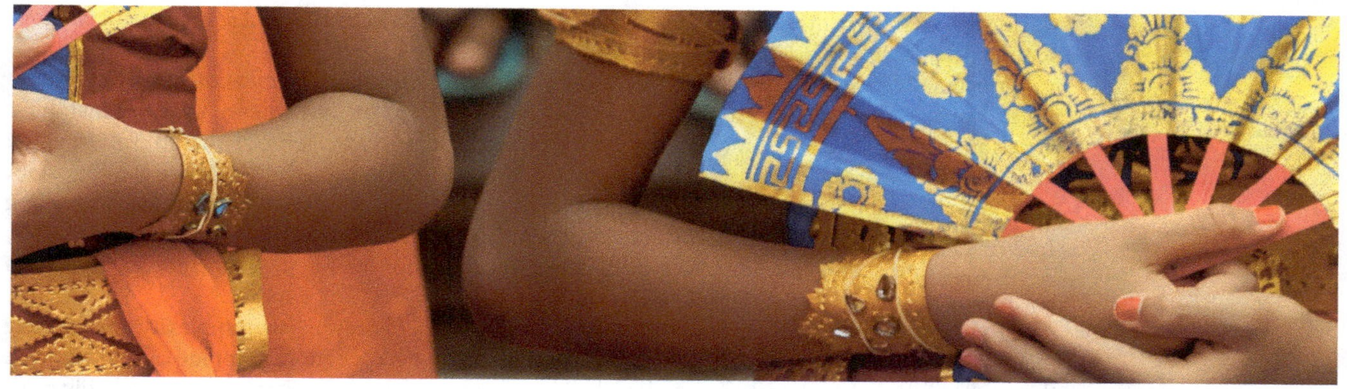

Chapter 1

Introduction to Anthropology

Let me tell you a story. No, as a matter of fact, let me tell you a number of stories through the course of this book, all of which are true as seen and remembered through the recorder or anthropologist's eyes. These are stories taken from ethnographic writings by researchers that are called Anthropologists. Anthropologists, as you can guess, study Anthropology and Anthropology is defined as the study of human societies and cultures and their development or as "the science that deals with the origins, physical and cultural development, biological characteristics, and social customs and beliefs of humankind" (https://www.dictionary.com/browse/anthropology).

In Anthropology, there are four subfields and these are known as physical or biological anthropology, cultural anthropology, archaeology, and linguistics. Each of these has its own definition depending upon the focus of study or research. Physical or biological anthropology can be defined as the study of the origins and evolution of human beings and how and why modern human populations vary biologically. Cultural anthropology can be defined as the study of the culture or customary ways of thinking and behaving in different societies. Linguistics is defined very broadly as the study of languages. Archaeology is defined as the study of past human societies and cultures and their changes through time.

In cultural Anthropology, generally you will see that people do ethnography defined as the systematic and scientific study of the way of life of one particular society. These studies include aspects of the society's subsistence, kinship patterns, economics, politics, and religion, from which many of the stories or case studies, as they are often referred to, come from for this book. Cultural Anthropologists also do ethnology that is defined as the comparative study of two or more societies. These studies are utilized to find general patterns of behaviors found in numerous societies, for instance, such as occurs with kinship patterns. Ethnologies utilize ethnographies that can be recorded as journal articles, field notes, or books. Today many of these sources of information are found online including at the Human Area Relation Files stored or managed at Yale University (http://hraf.yale.edu). Some cultural anthropologists specialize even within this field of study and there are also subfields of applied anthropology, medical anthropology, economic anthropology, the anthropology of law, anthropologists that study political ecology, and others. Specialists in the other subfields of physical anthropology, archaeology, and linguistics also may become highly focused in their research on issues related to forensic anthropology or historical linguistics or on areas of the world such as the Mediterranean, Mesoamerica, or the Andes Mountains where archaeologists concentrate their research, to name only a few.

Most of the case studies that we will review in this book are from cultural anthropologists studying and working with living peoples. These living peoples live in various types of societies that differ in various ways. Some of the major ways in which they differ include their population size, ways the society gets food or their subsistence strategies, and how complex the society is. These are important aspects to think about when studying people and societies since one can envision that they run along a continuum from less complex to more complex. The basic terms for these societies are bands, tribes, chiefdoms, and states with bands having less population and being less complex and states having much larger populations and being much more complex (Figure 1.1).

To understand these differences let's go ahead and find a definition for complexity. A good one that talks about some important aspects of societies as they become more complex can be found in the works of an archaeologist who studies the Nasca region of southern Peru, an area probably most famous for the "Nasca Lines." For Carmichael (1995: 181): "Complex societies are those in which hierarchically ordered social components exhibit marked functional differentiation and specialization. The components are therefore functionally interdependent in that no individual or group can fulfill all of the required roles and duties."

This is a good definition because it allows us to see how societies can change through time becoming either more complex or less complex. If a society is complex, it will have developed a hierarchy that means that the access to status, power, and wealth is unequal (Weber, 1968 [1922]). Max Weber, considered the father of modern day Sociology, indicated that in complex state-level societies you will find stratification, in that the population will be separated into two or more strata, with each strata including men, women, and children. This separation occurs in three areas: in status of individuals (prestige or esteem), in the power that they have (the ability to get people to do things), and in the wealth that they have (material assets and money). Stratified complex societies, therefore, will have different strata, classes, and/or castes of people indicated by this term hierarchy. In less complex societies, you will not find these strata or they will be much less well defined. In some less complex societies with little population, you may find no or very little differentiation between people in terms of status, wealth, and power and these societies are termed egalitarian.

The other aspect of this definition that helps us to understand what complex societies are is the concept of functional differentiation. This concept is linked to some Anthropologists' views that societies are comprised of parts that have structures and function to perform certain activities for the survival or continuation of the society (Evans-Pritchard, 1944; Malinowski, 1944, 1922; Radcliffe-Brown, 1952, 1933; Spencer, 1886). From this point of view, the evolution of society is based on its structural differentiation, which is dependent on, and determinant of its complexity (Stewart, 1955; White, 2007 [1959], 1969 [1949]). Well, actually it is not the part that has a function but it is the people that fill certain roles in a society and do certain jobs and perform certain activities that fulfill a need of the society or, actually, of the people in the society. Some of the basic needs

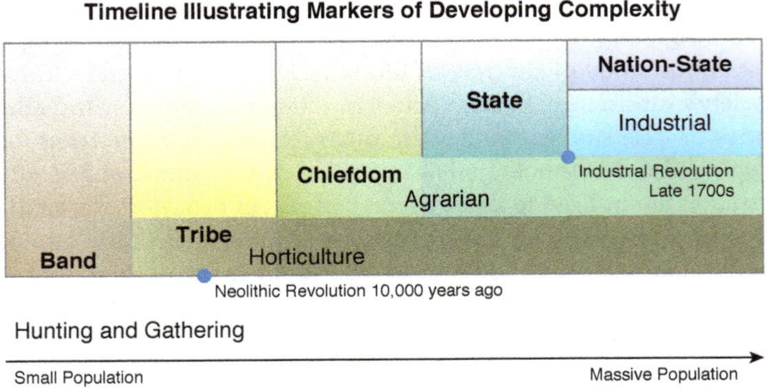

Figure 1.1 Aspects of the Development of Sociopolitical Complexity.
Source: developed from students' work at the Department of Anthropology, Sociology, and Social Work at Eastern Kentucky University

of people in societies include what we already mentioned such as subsistence, as well as marriage and biological and social reproduction, political leaders, religious practitioners, social control mechanisms, and health and education. All of these are functions that all societies have and in which people fulfill the different roles.

However, in less complex societies, the same person can fulfill many of these roles at the same time. For instance, in tribal societies there are religious practitioners called shaman who can communicate with the supernatural world in a religious function (Eliade, 1978, 1952). These same people can also be the political leaders of the groups to which they belong; they may also be farmers or hunters, all at the same time. As a society gets more complex, these functions become more differentiated and specialized. Each role becomes so specialized that no one person or group can fulfill all of the functions required by the different roles. Specialization becomes dominant but more so, structures within the society that develop in relation to these functions become differentiated to the point that they can become institutions of the society in their own right. When this occurs, each structure has a specific function in the society, that is, political or religious, and each individual focuses only on those roles. The institution is basically an entity running on its own internal rules and regulations but it must be linked to the other institutions of the society since each regulates different basic needs of individuals within that society. When you see hierarchies (stratification), institutions (of law, medicine, business, etc.), and highly specialized individual work, you are seeing a complex society.

Interestingly enough although billions of people today live in complex societies, there are many societies that are less complex today and this was true also especially in the past. Another way to envision this is to try to determine whether the kinship group itself is of key importance or if the individual is of key importance. Emile Durkheim (1947 [1893]) outlined these differences when he realized that societies could be organized around "mechanical solidarity" or "organic solidarity." If a society is organized around unifying principles of mechanical solidarity, then the organizing principles are based on kinship and the important entity that controls things and is perpetuated socially through time is the clan. A clan is an anthropological term indicating a compromise (the relationships are sometimes negotiated between people) kin group based on a rule of residence and a rule of descent. Individuals in a clan trace their descent back to a stipulated apical ancestor but they cannot actually demonstrate this and these ancestors are sometimes envisioned as nonhuman, which is called in Anthropology, a totem. This kinship group is how the individual gets their status, power, and wealth in these, what we might call "traditional" societies. Such traditional societies can and could be not very complex like bands or they could be ancient state-level societies, which still had unifying principles based on kinship that defined the individual's position within the hierarchy of the state. Durkheim noted that with industrialization these kinship structures have given way to organic solidarity or the principles of organization based on the specialization of the division of labor. In modern complex industrialized societies, one's position in that society is not based on kinship (though this certainly may have an affect) but is based on the individual and what the specialization of labor of the individual is. Also the individual has become the owner of the means and distribution of production, terms that come out of the work of Marx and Engels in studying changing economic structures (Marx, 1867; Marx and Engels, 1848). We should keep these things in mind as we go through the chapters on kinship, marriage, and descent patterns and then onto sociopolitical structures like ethnicity, states, and nation-states.

This outline of different societies is very broad but it gives us something to start with. The next thing we have to look at is the concept of culture, itself. This has been defined as simply as related to knowledge and beliefs that are learned (Tylor, 1871) or later in the twentieth century as being related to habits or behaviors that are learned and reproduced by the group (Boas, 1940, 1938 [1911]). Therefore, culture minimally is the information, attitudes, beliefs, and behaviors that we learn and pass on as a member of a society in a particular environment at a particular time period. Here we have to introduce some of the other theories for how to interpret culture and the numerous human societies in which it exists. In the Introduction to Anthropology textbooks, numerous theoretical orientations are usually listed and please see Bonzani (2016: Chapter 2) and Kottak (2013: 285—295) for an outline of these. For this book we are basically going to just look at those theories which deal with the structures found in all societies (structuralism; Lévi-Strauss 1967, 1966) and the functions of those structures (structural functionalism) and how these can change through place and time. We are also briefly going to look at ways to interpret activities within cultures such as rituals in relation to religion and the cycle of life (Van Gennep, 2004 [1908]), gift giving in relation to economics (Mauss, 1966 [1925]), and underlying meanings to actions (Geertz, 1973, 1963).

Of all of the different aspects of individuals' actions and interactions that could be addressed in this book or on any class on cultural diversity, we are going to focus on kinship interactions including marriage and descent and why kinship might be considered the cornerstone for the understanding of human societies or the study of Anthropology. In the second half of the book, we will cover how the concept of territoriality can help us understand sociopolitical entities and institutions. What are their basic forms or structures; how fluid or rigid might these structures be; and why these entities seem to act and interact in somewhat predictable ways regardless of the size of the society? These entities have been termed "imagined communities" (Anderson, 1983; Barth, 1969) and include the basic sociopolitical structures of bands, tribes, chiefdoms, and states. However, the term, "imagined communities," has also been utilized to encompass communities now termed indigenous peoples, ethnic groups and ethnicity, and nation-states, nationality, and nationalism, all of which will be covered in the second part of the book.

PART I

Why Does Kinship Seem to Be More Important to Some Societies and Who Cares Who You Marry Anyway?

Chapter 2

The Origins and Diversification of Sociopolitical Systems

At the Family Level: Kinship Practices and Marriage as Exchange

Kinship. Kinship is considered by some if not all Anthropologists as the key or cornerstone to all sociopolitical systems and development. All Anthropologists have to have some education and training in tracing kinship groups. Some of the best known Anthropologists have written foundational books on the subject including the French Anthropologist Claude Lévi-Strauss who wrote "The Elementary Structures of Kinship (Les structures élémentaires de la parenté)" (1969a) and "The Raw and the Cooked" (1969b) and Robin Fox who wrote "Kinship and Marriage" (1967).

These books are utilized to help to write this brief chapter on the topic of kinship. Another book by Beatrice Gottlieb (1993) also has given insight into marriage practices in Europe from the 1300s to the end of the 1800s. All of these text are utilized for the information and underlying hypotheses on the importance and meaning of the family and marriage and how these configurations change yet remain the same when one looks at the continuum of traditional to industrial societies that are discussed also in the next few chapters. My own studies at the University of Pittsburgh, where I took a class on kinship with Dr. Hugo Nutini, and then my travels in the Colombian Amazon with researchers, while they studied the clan systems of the Tikuna indigenous people in this region, have all lead to my own understandings of the importance and great fascination with this aspect of human societies.

Along with this training in Anthropology the sociopolitical systems of human societies also seem to be linked back to biology and the ideas of Charles Darwin (1859) and others in relation to the availability of resources, who controls them, and who does and does not have access to them. Sometimes, this is referred to as the struggle for existence or competition between species as populations can expand indefinitely except for a limitation on resources. Since individuals are the ones who reproduce, they seem to be a logical starting point for understanding this relationship between humans and the environments in which they live. By starting with the individual, we can see that to perpetuate themselves and their "Culture" or the norms and rules and behaviors which are held mainly in common by a group of people or society, reproduction both sexually (biological evolution) and socially (social reproduction) are important if we want to think of things in the long term or through time. One thing a lot of researchers will tell you is that nothing stays the same. Here is where the concept of marriage becomes important and where descent systems play such an integral part in the perpetuation of different sociopolitical systems.

These systems vary based on the population level of the society and this is usually intimately tied to how the society gets its food or its subsistence systems. As if looking at blocks that build one upon the other, we can start with the individual and then outline the next types of groups to which individuals belong. In a basic introductory Anthropology course, the family or nuclear family is the next, sometimes considered fundamental, level or building block for these systems. After this we can add other community arrangements that in the past and traditionally would include larger kinship structures. Expanding upon these, we could then add the basic larger political units that Anthropologists categorize in a simplistic way as bands, tribes, chiefdoms, and states. In a lecture these can be divided into three levels of integration or exclusion depending on the context. These levels can be listed as:

1. Family Level

   This level includes social institutions: kinship systems, marriage patterns, and descent groups.

2. Community Level

   This level includes aspects of the mechanisms for promoting egalitarianism, hierarchies, positions, or rights, and two other key concepts in Anthropology and for the understanding of the importance of kinship called ascribed and achieved positions in a society.

3. Intercommunity Level

   The relationships between communities are based on the diversity of arrangements that are graded or form an ever-changing continuum ranging from kinship to political and economic affiliations. These forms are bands, tribes, chiefdoms, states, and nation-states.

The social institutions listed under this first level of the family will be discussed and the terms defined in the following section of this chapter. These later two levels will be discussed in this book under PART II: Which Flag Should I Fly on the Fourth of July?

Family Level: The Kinship Basis of Social Evolution

What is kinship and why is it important? Many students can define kinship as your kin relations; the people you are related to and they are right. However, it is so much more than that and one does not usually think of these underlying important aspects of kinship but if we look at a basic definition of kinship one can see what I mean. Kinship can be defined as: The allocation of rights and their transmission from one generation to the next. These rights are as diverse as, for example, group membership, succession to office, inheritance of property, locality of residence, types of occupation, and other cultural aspects.

To those of us living in industrial societies, as will be discussed more so later, some of these allocations do not make much sense or do not seem to exist anymore. Aren't we all citizens of the world? Or aren't most of us living here in the United States citizens of the United States? Perhaps we really do not consider kinship as giving us group membership but, if you were born in the United States, thanks to your relationship to your parents, that gives you group membership to the United States. In other places if your parents are members of a particular tribe, indigenous and ethnic group, then that gives you membership also to that group. If your kinship does not give you that group membership then you are not part of that tribe, indigenous, ethnic group or even state.

What about succession to office? Well in many traditional and past societies, the only way one could be placed into a position of power (a political office) such as a chief or a king or queen was based on who you were related to. If you were in the family line from which the chiefs came or for that matter the kings and queens then, potentially, you could be the next king. However in democratic societies, which are often now industry based (Figure 2.1), this is illegal and is referred to as nepotism (*nepos* is Latin for nephew). This term comes from the idea of placing your nephew or son or close relative from

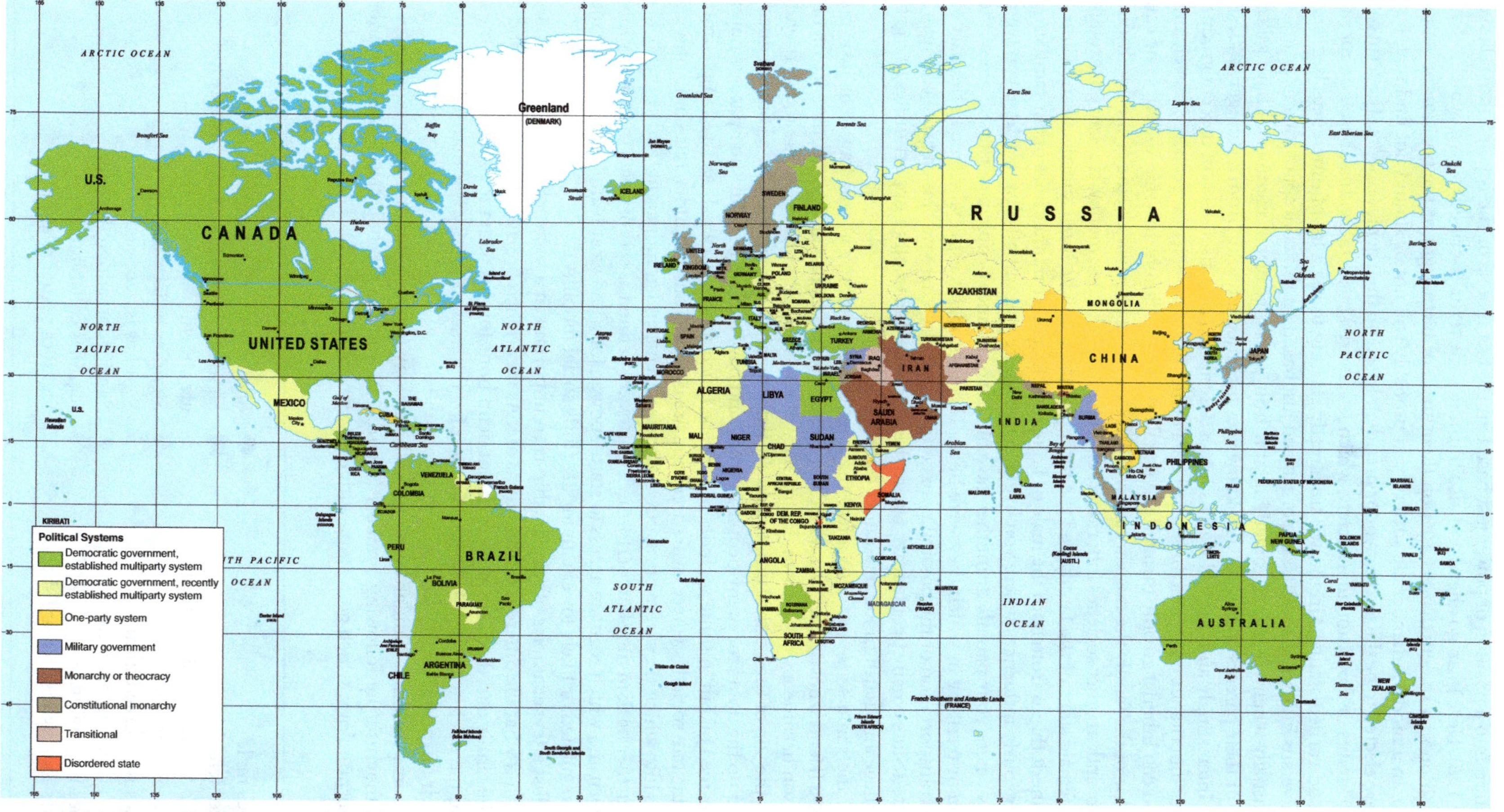

Figure 2.1 Political Systems of the World.

Key: Adapted from Allen, John L., and Audrey C. Shalinsky. *Student Atlas of Anthropology*. New York: McGraw-Hill Companies, 2004.

Map: ©dikobraziy/Shutterstock.com

the next generation into a position of power just based on the fact that he or she is your close relative (Gottlieb, 1993: 196). Here I can go ahead and also introduce the term "ascribed" status, which refers to a person's position in a society that is based on their birth, or birth-right or the position or status one is born into. In a modern democratic society, you probably will not or should not find that, but instead people are elected to be the next mayor or president based on their achievements. The term for this is "achieved" status or a position in a society, which is acquired by an individual, based on merit, achievements, and earned status. Alright, we are already starting to see a lot of differences between how traditional versus industrial societies are organized just based on this concept of kinship.

To go on, usually when we inherit something, it is from a relative or kin members. I have asked students if they or their parents or anyone they know ever inherited anything from a stranger; and, so far, no one has. Interestingly and this will lead us into a description and discussion of descent groups, in some societies inheritance only goes through the male line. In some societies, property, power, and titles (things you can inherit) go only through the female side of the family. In some societies one can choose which side of the family the nuclear family will follow and hence which side of the family one will inherit from; and, in other societies inheritance of property, land, titles, money, etc., can go through both male and female sides of the family and the terms for these will be listed shortly. In the United States we can inherit things from both the male or father and female or mother lines of our families.

Kinship obviously influences where you live because where you initially live is where you were born and that is where your parents or mother gave birth. Sometimes people never move out of the general location or territory in which they were born. This is probably especially true in the past or in areas where transportation or the possibility of getting a job elsewhere was much reduced. Again, here in the United States many people leave where they grew up due to other opportunities like getting to go to college and getting a job in another state.

Kinship in the same sense can also affect the type of occupation you will have. For just one example, I have a friend whose father was a medical doctor. He had a great and good influence on his family and his son became a well- known doctor, a cardiologist. The last time I spoke to my friend, the daughter of the son of their father is now a medical doctor also. Here in the United States education has opened up the doors for many people to study and have careers in fields their parents never would have dreamed of, but in some societies this can be much more restricted. As an example from Anthropology in state societies where castes were and are common such as India, one could only do the occupations into which they were born and that their parents and grandparents and probably kin relatives even further back in time had performed. Castes are defined as sets of strata in a society into which one is born and which regulate access to status, power, jobs, and wealth and in which a person is pretty much regulated or likely to remain for life (little social mobility).

Those are just a few examples of why kinship is so important in a society. If we go on then, we have to understand what the different kinship units are. As mentioned previously, the key or foundational unit is the family and there are a few different definitions for this with the main one and most common being the nuclear family. A basic definition for the nuclear family is a married man and woman and their offspring.

There are some common standard ways in Anthropology to graph this and other kinship relationships and they use the following symbols (Figure 2.2) and the symbols have some common classificatory terminology, which goes along with each symbol (Figure 2.3).

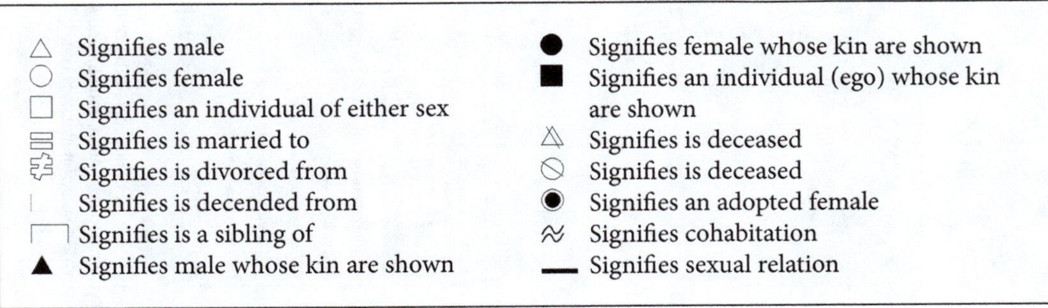

Figure 2.2 Common Symbols Used in Kinship Charts.

Primary Kin Types		Usages	
father	Fa	F	F
mother	Mo	M	M
husband	Hu	H	H
wife	Wi	W	W
brother	Br	B	B
sister	Si	Z	S
son	So	S	s
daughter	Da	D	d

Figure 2.3 Common Kinship Terms of Primary Kin.

Now if we look at this definition we see two important aspects to the definition (Figure 2.4). The first is the concept of marriage or being married. This aspect has a biological aspect and a cultural aspect. Therefore, being considered married in one place or society might not be the same as in another. In some societies like in the Pacific Islands, you are not considered married until after you add "board to bed" and a man and woman become a couple and can have a common residence but are not considered married until families of both partners recognize this fact (Ward, 2005: 30). In other societies like in the United States, you are not considered to be married unless you have a license issued by the local justice of the peace or legal system in which you live. Even in the same society you might have a legal marriage license but some people might not consider that you are married until you go to a religious location like a church and are married in the eyes of the Lord. From this we can see that marriage is between two individuals but it also involves the communities in which one lives. Therefore, in many places in the world, marriage is not just the love between two individuals and their union as "one" but also the union of the families and communities to which the individuals belong.

Here we can introduce the concepts of consanguinity and affinity. Consanguinity relates to "blood" relations, those people to which you are related based on blood or genetics. Your parents and your children are your consanguineal relatives. Now adopted children can be considered as part of the family because humans can and have developed things that are called fictive relations. You may not be the blood/genetics son or daughter of your parents but you still are their children. Your affines or affinity refers to your relatives that you have gained based on marriage, relatives through marriage. For your father, his wife's (your mother) relatives are his affines and these relationships are of extreme importance because they build reciprocal relations between otherwise different descent groups. Many important chiefs or kings of large territories have been able to become "kings" because they have been able to build alliances through marriage, by marrying the daughter of another important person or chief or by having the daughter of an important person marry the son of an important person. Never underestimate the power of alliances and building reciprocal relations. Clear examples

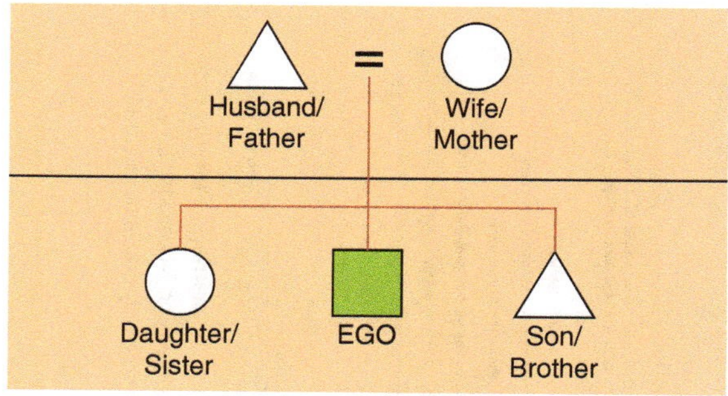

Figure 2.4 Kinship Chart of the Nuclear Family Defined as a Married Man and Woman and Their Offspring.

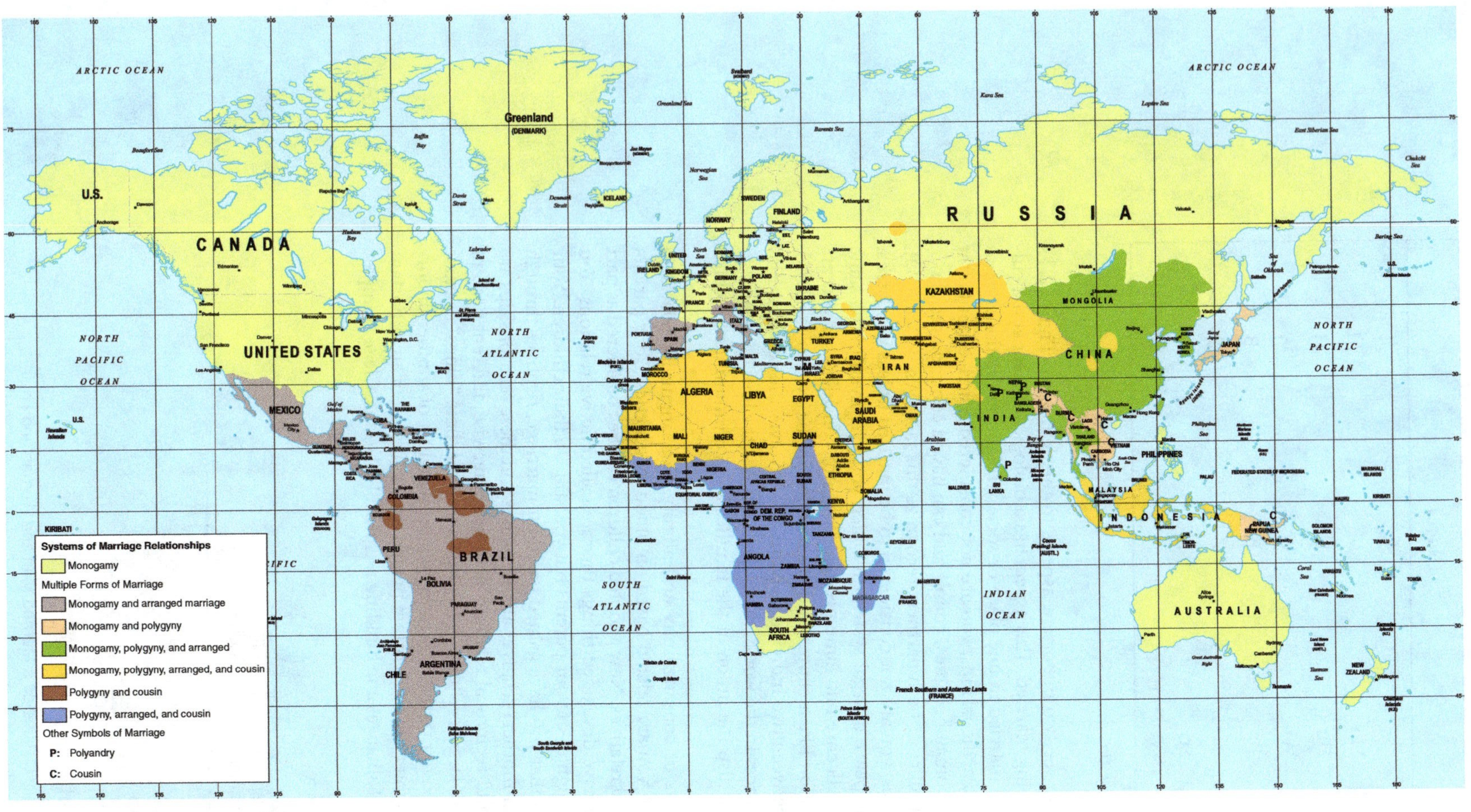

Figure 2.5 Marriage Patterns Around the World.
Key: Adapted from Allen, John L., and Audrey C. Shalinsky. *Student Atlas of Anthropology*. New York: McGraw-Hill Companies, 2004.
Map: ©dikobraziy/Shutterstock.com

of this process at work are referred to in Anthropology as arranged marriages. Now again this is very rare in the United States where individuals have a lot of people they can chose from with whom to marry and we often marry for "love;" however, many societies around the world practice arranged marriages (Figure 2.4) where we can see the importance of affinity, reciprocal relations, alliances, joining territories into one family.

Why does this all of a sudden when people get married become one family when before it was two? Well, obviously that is where biology comes in and the second important aspect of the definition of a nuclear family. Remember that the definition is a married man and woman and their offspring. The offspring is what in time will make this one family and not two. The man and woman, the family of the man and the family of the woman become one when the children are born. They carry on not only the biology and genes of their respective parents and families, but they carry on the "name of the family" and the sociocultural norms, responsibilities and privileges, and behavioral practices that they learn from their parents, families, and communities that are passed on through time. Very important.

Now does it always have to be a married man and woman that makes up a family and in Anthropology we see that the answer is no and so you will also find a number of other terms that define a family. Also distantly related and/or nonrelated persons may also make up the family or what is sometimes referred to as the "house" or household. For instance, cousins, nephews and nieces, or other "visiting" (in quotations because these visits are not just for three days [I have heard a saying that relatives can visit for three days but after that they start to smell like fish, or something like that] but may extend into months or years) relatives may be part of the house and live in the household; nonrelated members may be servants in one form or the other that are considered part of the house.

In terms of definitions, first is the minimal nuclear unit that consists of the mother and offspring. To understand this definition, we also have to know something about Physical Anthropology and general biology and specifically reproductive biology. In reproductive biology of males and females, there are obviously differences. These differences are also found in other animals, like other primates, which humans are classified as. In other words when you have to place humans into a classificatory scheme with other animals, we physically and physiologically and, also we know now genetically, are more similar to chimpanzees (that are noted to be human's closest related other species), great apes, and orangutans than we are to, let's say, cats and dogs. Sounds pretty obvious. Primatologists that study other primates note that humans and these other primates have certain behaviors that they share in common. One of these is mating practices or strategies. Another is called territoriality and we will discuss that in Part II.

Mating practices. Sounds pretty interesting and it is. Because of reproductive biology and the differences between males and females, human women can only have one or more rarely two children in an approximate nine-month time period. However, men can have as many children in the same approximate time period as they can get women pregnant. For now we are just talking about biology. In terms of reproductive success (the more offspring you have that survive and let's say go on into adulthood to have their own children) the better. For men that would mean the more women you can mate with in a given amount of time, the more likely you will have numerous offspring and that is what reproductive success seems to mean for males: put another way males compete for mates to mate with. Now for females they can mate with as many males or men as a man could with women in the same amount of time, but they will always only have one or two children in a nine-month time span. Because of this in biology, biologists and primatologists indicate that while males compete for many mates, females compete for a mate with a lot of resources. If you can only mate with one male, why not make it be one that has a lot of resources that will be able to ensure the success of the child you will have anyway? This reasoning or explanation also seems to be linked to the explanation that in many societies men do have more than one wife or at least it is allowed in those societies if the man has enough resources to take care of the additional wives and children, while in very few societies will you find women having more than one husband at the same time (see Figure 2.4). The terms for marriage practices in Anthropology in relation to these concepts include monogamy, the marriage of one man to one women at the same time; polygamy including polygyny when one man is married to more than one women at the same time and polyandry when one women is married to more than one man at the same time; and serial monogamy when a person is married, gets divorced and then marries another person but not at the same time. So back to the definition of a minimal nuclear unit and the reason why it is the mother and offspring and not the father and offspring. The reason is that generally if one of the parents leaves the unit, it will be the man who may often have the opportunity to mate with another female and have more children.

Other terms related to the family include the extended family and the family by choice. The extended family is when in a household or house unit a nuclear family or mother and children live with their grandparents, or a sister and her husband and children live in the same household, or some other permutation where lineal relatives (those related through descent) also live with lateral relatives (those of the same generation) in the same household. For a family by choice this is the term usually describing male—male relationships or female—female relations that form a union to make a family. These unions can include children also perhaps biologically by one of the partners or through adoption by the two partners. Here again we see the concept of a union, for various reasons like sexual, economic, companionship, support. Depending on the community within a society in which the partners live, this can be considered a marriage, such as if a marriage license has been issued to the couple as occurs in some places in the United States but not in others. Also children and the perpetuation of the partners' families can be part of a family by choice.

Before we go onto the different marriage patterns, let's cover the types of descent systems that are found in human societies. For all of the people in the world, one might think that there would be an endless number of types of descent systems and this would also apply to the types of marriage patterns; however, there are only three types of inheritance rules that lead to four basic types of descent systems. The three types of inheritance rules are primogeniture, patrilineal inheritance, and matrilineal inheritance. Primogeniture refers to inheritance that goes through the first born son. Patrilineal inheritance refers to inheritance that goes through the line of the male and matrilineal inheritance refers to inheritance that goes through the line of the female.

Notice the use of the preposition "through." In many traditional societies today and in the past, it is the kinship group that controls resources such as land. The individual first-born son does/did not actually own the inheritance or land but controlled it. Therefore, it was not like a free for all party for the first-born son. In fact, in the will of the father or mother in Europe where primogeniture inheritance was found from the 1300s to 1800s, it could be stipulated that he would have to give his brothers and sisters some form of income for their upkeep. Think of this more as a system of stewardship (Gottlieb, 1993: 201—227) in societies where the sociopolitical systems are organized around the kinship group and clan (referred to as ancestor-focused or as Durkheim [1947] called it mechanical solidarity) as opposed to societies that are organized around the division of labor or the individual (referred to as ego-focused or as Durkheim [1947] called it organic solidarity) (Fox, 1967: 163—164; Goodenough, 1951). Inheritance through the male line's meaning is pretty obvious as inheritances that pass through males in a family. Inheritance through the female line's meaning is also obvious as inheritances that pass through the females of the family.

From these inheritance rules, then Anthropologists have found four primary systems of descent. These are defined as unilineal of which there are patrilineal societies or matrilineal societies (Figures 2.6 and 2.7), bilineal societies (Figure 2.8), and ambilineal societies. In unilineal systems of descent, inheritance only passes through one sex either the male or the female. To inherit pretty much anything in these societies, you have to be part of the family and you have to be the same sex through which inheritances pass. Usually we find that tribal, chiefdom, and preindustrial state societies practice unilineal descent and they can be horticultural or pastoral or agricultural in the manner in which they obtain food. In a following chapter for Part I, a short case study based on ethnographies and ethnologies will be presented to give you an idea of different descent systems and marriage patterns.

This is very interesting because while you are doing Anthropology and talking to an informant or helper or friend in one of these societies, you may start to notice that the person calls a number of people by the term mother or by the term father, depending on the language. This is very different from our society here in the United Sates where, basically, we only call one person mother or father, though we may also have a stepfather or stepmother. We do not call our aunts mothers. This is because in unilineal descent system societies, the wife or the husband will also move to the village or town and even into or close by to the family of the wife or husband. If the bride moves to the husband's kin household or village, it is referred to as patrilocal or virilocal marriage residence patterns

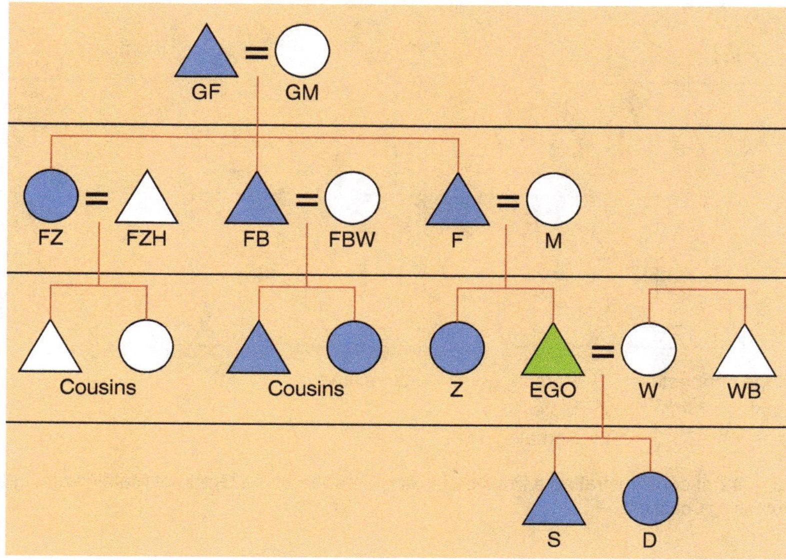

Figure 2.6 Patrilineal Descent Patterns Illustrating Descent Traced through the Male Line.

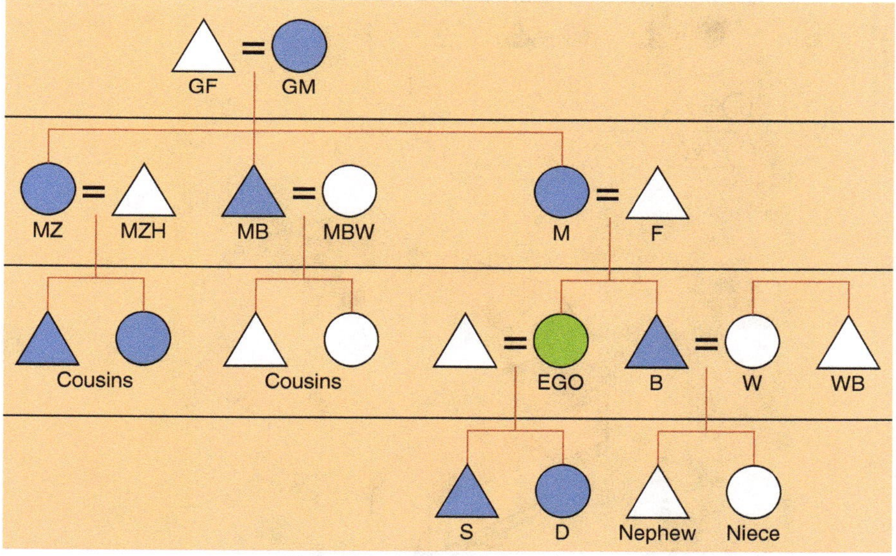

Figure 2.7 Matrilineal Descent Patterns Illustrating Descent Traced through the Female Line.

(Figure 2.9); if the husband moves to the bride's family household or village, it is referred to as matrilocal or uxorilocal marriage residence patterns. However sometimes in matrilineal societies, it has been found that the sons of a couple may move in with their maternal uncle and then when the son gets married, his wife moves in or they move close by this maternal uncle. In this case we must remember that inheritance passes through the female, but her male brothers always remain important to the extended family. This pattern is referred to as avunculocal marriage residence pattern and seems to occur as horticultural societies come under stress for competition for land, for instance, and when the likelihood of intergroup violence increases. In this case the reasoning goes that it is probably a good idea to have your male relatives close by to fend off any raiding or feuding enemies (Figure 2.10).

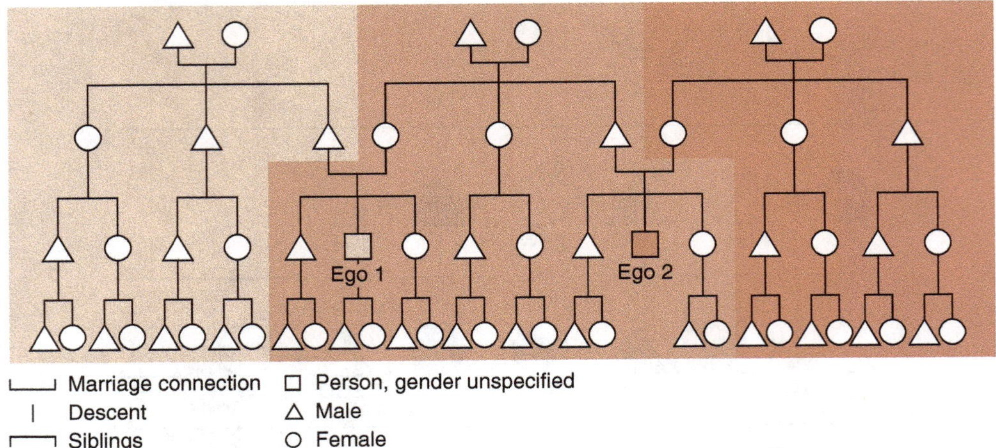

Figure 2.8 Bilineal Descent Illustrating a Practice Linking Persons with a Group of Matrilineal and Patrilineal Ties.
©Kendall Hunt Publishing Company

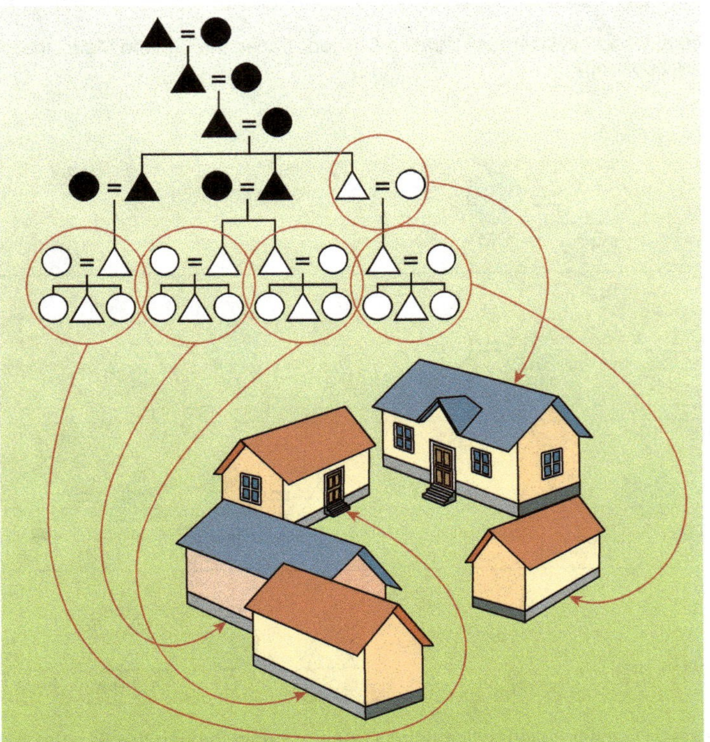

Figure 2.9 Patrilocal or Virilocal Marriage Residence Pattern.
©Kendall Hunt Publishing Company

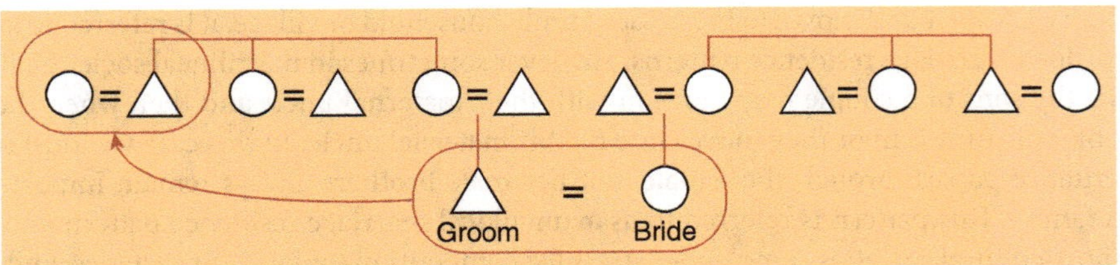

Figure 2.10 Avunculocal Marriage Residence Pattern.
©Kendall Hunt Publishing Company

Thereby, this movement makes people in a village or town often very closely related so that your father's brothers who live in the same town and very close to your father, all basically help you like a father and hence are called by the same term. Women of the same generation may also be called by the same term of mother since they act like your mother to care for you and provide for you and teach you things. This terminology system is called bifurcate merging kinship terminology (Figure 2.11).

Another one of the descent systems, referred to as bilineal, means that inheritance can pass through both males and females and not only one or the other. In the United States, that is the descent system you will typically find whereby one can inherit money, land, and other things through both their father and mother and you can be male or female to inherit. This type of descent does occur in complex state-level societies and is often associated to a terminology system referred to as lineal kinship terminology system whereby your mother, father, mother's and father's sisters, and mother's and father's brothers have different kinship terms. This may be the case because in these systems the bride and groom will often move into their own households when they get married and do not move in

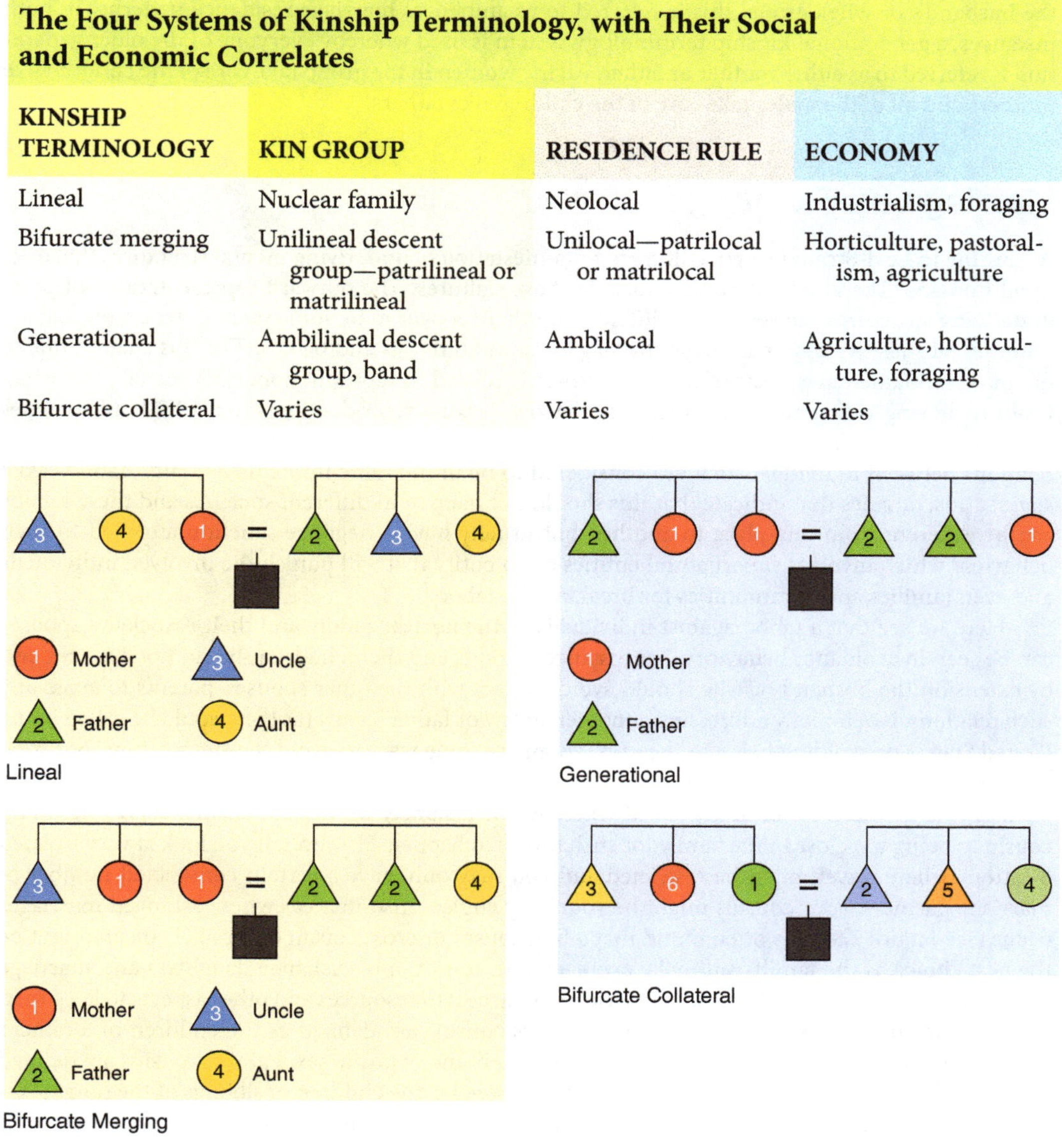

The Four Systems of Kinship Terminology, with Their Social and Economic Correlates

KINSHIP TERMINOLOGY	KIN GROUP	RESIDENCE RULE	ECONOMY
Lineal	Nuclear family	Neolocal	Industrialism, foraging
Bifurcate merging	Unilineal descent group—patrilineal or matrilineal	Unilocal—patrilocal or matrilocal	Horticulture, pastoralism, agriculture
Generational	Ambilineal descent group, band	Ambilocal	Agriculture, horticulture, foraging
Bifurcate collateral	Varies	Varies	Varies

Figure 2.11 The Four Systems of Kinship Terminology and Economic and Social Correlates.

with the husband's or wife's families. This type of residence marriage pattern is called neolocal. Here we can see that if you live in your own household with just your parents around, perhaps far away from either of the parent's families, it is not very likely that you are going to consider your uncle as being the same or have the same activities and behaviors toward you as your father does who actually lives with you. That would be the same with your aunts, who maybe every Christmas you might see, but they are certainly not like your mother. Also in some very complex societies each relative seems to perform a different role and you may find that father, mother, and the sisters and brothers of your father, and the sisters and brothers of your mother all have different terms. This classificatory system is referred to as bifurcate collateral kinship terminology.

The other descent system is also very interesting and is referred to as ambilineal descent system. In this case the person or couple can choose which side of the family they would like to trace descent from. From ethnographies for instance of hunter-gatherer groups in southern Africa (Lee, 1979), these types of descent systems are often associated to hunter-gatherer groups or bands that move around a lot. In this case the nuclear family may decide to move around with the husband's family or they may decide to move with the mother's family. When married partners live with either the husband's or wife's group, this is referred to as ambilocal marriage residence patterns. In both instances, a generational kinship terminology system is used whereby everyone of the older generation is referred to as either mother or father. All the women in the group take care of the children like mothers and all of the males take care of the children like fathers.

Marriage as Exchange

According to Levi-Straus (1969), culture is a manifestation of underlying mental structures that exist in all humans. Therefore, all human societies have cultures. The outward representations of these underlying structures can seem very different but there appear to be some mental structures that are found in all societies that may shape the way humans do things and behave. For this chapter one of the most fundamental aspects of these structures is related to reproduction, both sexual and social. From reviewing different social practices related to sexual reproduction (Fox, 1967), all societies have an underlying rule which is related to a prohibition against incest. Incest is defined as sexual relations between individuals that are considered to be in the same immediate family. Taboos exist against this, or rules that indicate that this should not happen in different societies and these taboos can be different from one place to another, but usually have a negative sanction attached to such behaviors which involves supernatural entities or an entity that will punish the involved individuals and even families and communities for breaking the taboo.

Here we see that a taboo against individuals in the nuclear family and their associated spouses can be seen in avoidance behaviors. For instance, parents and their children should not have sex and by extension the husband or wife should avoid contact with the other spouses' parents to avoid any such relations. Not directly addressing a mother-in law or father-in law (as they would be called in the United States) or avoiding being in the same room are some ways to avoid the "temptation" of sexual relations with a close relative. Well what about cousins? Here again the normalcy or commonness of marrying a cousin is culturally based whereby, for instance, we might consider marrying a first cousin as being too close in the family for such things to happen. However, if you look at very isolated locations where travel might be restricted and you may only have a certain constricted number of marriage partners, your cousins might be your only choice. Also in areas where arranged marriages occur (see Figure 2.5), it is often found that a first cousin or cross cousin or parallel cousin might be the best choice as the family can make arrangements to not only exchange daughters and marriage partners, but they can also then use territories, have access to resources and other aspects to keep such resources within the larger extended family. Cross cousins are defined as the children of a father's sister or of a mother's brother, i.e. children of siblings of the opposite sex. Parallel cousins are defined as the children of a father's brother and a mother's sister, i.e. the children of siblings of the same sex.

In these instances, daughters are considered to be exchanged and the cases are referred to as restricted marriage exchange as opposed to generalized marriage exchange where any number of individuals in different families can be married. In the restricted marriage exchanges, often cross

	BRIDEWEALTH PAYMENTS	*DOWRY*
Content	Movable property	All property
Recipients	Kin of the bride	Bride
Givers	Kin of groom	Kin of bride
Returnability	Usually	Always
Payable	Over time	At marriage
Use	Societal fund	Family fund

Figure 2.12 Types of Exchanges Found in Marriages.

cousins in restricted family arrangements are married; and, in a more elaborate form, you might see preferential sister exchanges where one daughter marries their cross cousin and the daughter of the other family then marries her cross cousin which would be the brother of the first married daughter. The reason this is not considered incest to these societies is that because of descent, the cross cousins can be considered to be of different descent groups and not of the same immediate family. For instance, in patrilineal descent societies, descent is traced through the male line; the children of the father trace descent to his father: so does his brother and his children, and so does his sister. However, here is the difference from bilineal societies like in the United Sates where we trace descent through both the mother and father. The children of the father's sister are his children's cross cousins but they do not trace descent through their mother, but do so through their father and, thereby, are not considered to be of the same family line or descent group as the children of the sister's brother. They are from different families; it is not incest; and it further builds reciprocal relations between groups who probably live in nearby territories and would like to continue to use similar resources through time into the future. This same scenario would work in matrilineal societies if descent was traced only through the female line. Therefore not only in many places of the world are marriages arranged, but you will often find people married to their cousins (see Figure 2.5). In the United Sates and especially with internet dating, you really are not restricted much in terms of your potential mating and marriage partners unlike in many nonindustrial or traditional societies in the past and even today around the world.

Not only are people involved in these exchanges but land, household goods, money, and other objects can be exchanged. The terms for these exchanges include bride wealth or bride price, dowries, and bride service (Figure 2.12). For bride wealth, one usually sees this in patrilineal societies with patrilocal residence patterns where the bride leaves her home to move into the house of her husband or his families' village. To replace the loss of the daughter for the family from which she is leaving, the groom and his kinship group will give her family bride wealth. This is usually in the form of some moveable property that can be moved to her family or families' village. The exchange of cattle by the Nuer is one example of this where the groom and his kin, give the bride's family a certain number of cattle (Evans-Pritchard, 1940). If for some reason the marriage wants to be broken later on, here in the United States that is called a divorce, the bride wealth should be returned and negotiations between the two families will ensue. Sometimes this happens because the new husband and wife do not have children and another marriage arrangement is desired by the husband's family in hopes of having future grandchildren and especially male children to pass on the family name and continue the patrilineal descent system.

On the other hand, as is often found in bilineal societies even in the United States, the bride will have accumulated a dowry from her family, which she takes with her upon marriage. The dowry often includes important household items or objects passed down to her from her family, like a handmade quilt from her grandmother. It can also include land or money and if the marriage is broken or a divorce takes place, she can usually retain control over the property she brought into the marriage so that it can eventually be passed on to her children from the first marriage or if she has children from a later marriage. For bride service, the groom works for the bride's family for a certain amount of time before and sometimes even after they are married. This type of exchange has been noted in hunter-gatherer groups where the children may have been arranged to be married at a young age and the groom/husband helps her family hunt for food, for instance.

Other terms that we use in Anthropology to account for the exchange aspect of marriage as occurring between families is the levirate and sororate. Again, these are practices that are very uncommon in the United States and in industrial societies where individuals have more say over who they marry and are often not living with either the groom's or bride's families. The levirate is when a man marries his dead brother's widow and the sororate is when a woman marries her dead sister's widower. Here in the United States we might ask how in the world can that happen as we would think that is very strange for our mother to marry our father's brother if he passed away or for our father to marry our aunt if our mother passed away. Well think of this example, for instance as recorded ethnographically for the Jivaro of the Amazonia in Ecuador (Harner, 1973). In a patrilineal—patrilocal society, the wife has moved into the village of her husband. She has left her own home and village and may visit but probably would not return to live there. Especially if children have been born, she and her children are now part of her husband's family. For some indigenous groups raiding of other groups was not uncommon and the Jivaro were known to have raided for heads or the power that the death and head would accrue into the family and wives of the head-hunter. Of course, these practices, as you can image, can be very dangerous and let's say that the husband is killed in one of these raids. The wife and children cannot really return to her family and village. Her husband's family is surely not going to kick them out into the forest and there was no state-level welfare system in place at the time. Under these circumstances, one solution is for the dead husband's brother to marry his now widowed wife and take care of her and her children.

On the other hand, let's say that a daughter is married to a man and the family receives bride wealth to replace her loss and she dies before having any children. The marriage is between two people but it is also between the families so the hope was that the married couple would have children again to perpetuate the social group. No children were born so the husband's family might ask for the return of the bride wealth. Many things could have happened since the two individuals were married like the bride wealth was already used or spent or traded by the wife's family and it would be very difficult for them to return it. Another option would be to have one of the sisters of the dead wife marry her widower; and, thereby, his family and he get a new bride and the dead wife's family gets to retain the bride wealth. If we think of these exchanges in this way, they make a lot more sense.

Finally, one might notice that sometimes in a society a person has to marry outside of their group or in some instances or societies, one has to marry within their group. The anthropological terms for this are exogamy and endogamy. Exogamy involves rules which require a person to marry outside of their respective group such as immediate family, clan, and moiety. On the other hand, endogamy involves rules where one must marry within the group into which they were born, perhaps the tribe, indigenous group or religion, or caste. Since these are rules that are utilized to perpetuate the kin group through time, they can be strictly enforced. In the Amazon of Colombia we met a Tikuna man who had married outside of the Tikuna indigenous group and married a Peruvian woman with no tribal affiliations. Because of this, he said he could no longer lay claim to any of the rights of being Tikuna including the use of commonly held land. Sometimes, for instance, in more remote areas of India where one must marry within their caste, if two individuals that are from different castes elope, the elders may send people after them to punish them for breaking such rules. The elopement or marriage will not be recognized by the community and a negative sanction as severe as death might be enforced. Here in the United Sates if you eloped in the past or had to today, your parents might all be mad at you but it is unlikely that they would send someone after you to punish you, and especially with death!

Hence, this is cultural diversity that one might find in different societies in relation to kinship and marriage practices. In the next chapter, we have to go over a brief history of the industrial revolution to try to understand why industrial societies like the United States seem to be different from other traditional or nonindustrial societies when it comes to marriage practices and other sociopolitical structures like types of economic, religious, and political systems.

Chapter 3

Factors Fueling the Industrial Revolution and Technology, Population Growth, and Economics

One way that marriage patterns are noted to be different in industrial societies is that they often involve neolocal marriage residence patterns. This pattern gives us a clue as to important differences between societies in which one's position is based on kinship and societies in which one's position is based on a division of labor or on individual's achievements, let's say. In neolocal residence marriage patterns, when a couple gets married, they move out of both spouses' parents households and establish their own household. This is common in industrial societies like in the United States because the individual will often leave their homes to go to college or leave their homes to go to work someplace on their own, not often related to what and where their parents do or live. This type of marriage pattern apparently also did occur in preindustrial Europe, for instance in the 1500s (Gottlieb, 1993), but by that time the seeds of industrialization were already beginning to grow, in relation to changes in the importance of the individual and social, economic, and political relations. To understand this a little bit better, let's go back in time and go over a brief history of the Industrial Revolution. We will see that the Industrial Revolution has a definite definition, starting time, and has gone through a number of phases. To go into more depth on these issues one should see Braudel's work (1981 [1979]) on civilization and capitalism in the 15th through 18th centuries of Europe.

One of the first thing Braudel (1981 [1979]) discusses in his book is about what were the population levels in Europe and China from about the 1300s to the 1800s. This is important because we can see that there was a slow increase overall in population levels in these areas followed by a rapid rise in population after about the mid-1700s. One might wonder why populations started to increase rapidly after about the 1720s and why this is important.

To obtain this type of information is difficult and one has to look at things like birth and death records in church parishes or in town archives and the information can be scarce and take a long time to find. However, the general trend of increasing population is born out even though there were sharp downturns in population between the 1350s and 1450s and again between 1650 and 1850.

In the 1300s and 1400s Europe was hit by the Black Death or the Bubonic Plague that is reported to have killed approximately 45 percent of all people in Europe if not more during this time period. Populations rebounded and estimates indicate that European population rose from 250 to 350 million people in the 1300s and doubled to ca. 700 million by 1780. In China a similar increase in population has been recorded to have occurred whereby in the 1680's population is estimated to be about 120 million and by 1850 it had reached 430 million, a three- to four-fold increase. Most of this increase in population is noted to be due to an increase in agricultural production and more food leading to more people. The reason for this agricultural production increase was the advent of new technologies such as the plow (Figure 3.1) which can more efficiently break up the soils for planting then could other technologies at the time like digging sticks.

Again it is like a feedback loop where when there is a lot of food, one can feed more people, and this allows for more children to be born. However as all feedback loops go, when there are more children, then you need more food to feed them and some scholars like Boserup (1966), in contradiction to other scholars on population growth like Thomas Malthus (Charbit and SpringerLink, 2009), felt that population pressure in an area pushes or leads to an increase in technological innovation. Perhaps you have heard the saying: "Necessity is the mother of invention" and that is what that means. When you really need something, you will try and figure out a way to achieve or acquire what you need. For food production systems, then, we can say as a population becomes denser, the means or strategy of production should shift from ones of low-energy input such as hunting and gathering, to extensive agriculture (i.e., slash-and-burn agriculture), to very intensive forms of agriculture that can feed a dense population.

At this time then in the 1500s to 1800s populations were growing in Europe. The development of the printing press which was a system of movable type, probably invented by Johannes Gutenberg,

Figure 3.1 Renditions of the development of the plow.
©Hennadii H/Shutterstock.com

in the middle of the fifteenth century (1400s) also occurs and allows for the dissemination of lots of information including on religion but also on mathematics and sciences which are necessary for technological instructions. This type of information is more easily and efficiently spread to the masses of the people who can make their own inventions as individuals with the skills to do so. Growing populations, the need for more food, and the spread of scientific thought (i.e., mathematics) in Europe then lead to a slow process starting in the 1400s to 1500s that sets the framework for the Industrial Revolution.

What is the Industrial Revolution? To be specific in the sense of the definition, the term "Industrial Revolution" refers to the dramatic technological and economic innovations that occurred in England during the period from about CE 1760 to 1830. A good definition can be found in Nolan and Lenski (2006:193): "To be meaningful, the term should be limited to *the period during which the productive activities of societies were rapidly transformed by the invention of a succession of machines powered by newer, inanimate sources of energy, such as coal, electricity, petroleum, and natural gas.*" Again we see a few aspects in this definition that allow us to understand what an industrial society is and help us to compare changes that have occurred in industrial societies to sociopolitical aspects of societies that are not industrial or are in the process of industrializing. First of all, we should keep in mind that this (industrialization) is a relatively new phenomenon in that it basically only started to occur since the 1760s. No societies anywhere in the world were industrial prior to this time period, so we should expect to see some big changes in family structures, sociopolitical structures, and economic structures in these times and in these industrial societies.

What are these changes? Before we can outline these changes, we still need to address the important aspects of this definition and we will go through the stages of industrialization up to the present. In the definition we see that industrial societies have machines that do labor more efficiently than humans. This is unlike in other types of societies like bands, tribes, chiefdoms, and agrarian states of the past and today where energy is supplied only by human labor or animal power (Table 3.1). These machines are more efficient or, in other words, a tractor can plow more land in less time than could just a human and thereby more food can be generated in less land.

The other aspect of the definition that we must keep our eyes on is that these machines are powered by at the time newer forms of energy including coal, petroleum, gasoline, and electricity. All of these except for electricity that can be generated from water are nonrenewable sources of energy; so a goal for humankind in the future has to be to find alternative sources of fuel that are renewable like solar power or electric run cars or other recyclable/renewable products that can produce energy. Clearly, when the nonrenewable sources of energy run out, we do not want to go back to the days before machines if only because without these efficient forms of producing goods and especially food, we will not be able to feed the now over 7 billion people on the earth. If we go back to the earlier discussions in the chapter on population and note that ca. 700 million people lived in Europe in the 1700s and 430 million people lived in China in the 1800s, adding that up to ca. 1.13 billion people by 1860 (not counting other parts of the world so we could say ca. 2 billion people on the earth in the late 1800s), we see that only in the last 150 years world population has increased more than three fold to ca. 7 billion people. Here I like to say we must be doing something right and what it seems to be is human's ability to invent new technologies and machines that are highly efficient and allow us to support so many people.

Let's go through the phases of the Industrial Revolution now.

The First Phase of the Industrial Revolution

As indicated by Braudel (1981 [1979]), the first phase of the Industrial Revolution occurred in England and was centered on the textile industry between CE 1770 and 1845. Water, food, shelter, clothing, education, and health care, are the basic necessities of all humans. Making cloths can start with spinning yard and a spinning wheel (Figure 3.2) and this can be seen as low-level production for the household but if production expends and needs for the community and even noncommunity members are to be accommodated, one needs more efficient means of making clothing.

Table 3.1 Changes in Socioeconomic Systems with the Shift from Cottage Industries to Factory-Run Industries.

Types of Society	Energy Source	Control of Production	Location of Production	Exchange Mechanism	Payment for labor	Political Institution	Religious Ideologies
Hunter-gatherer	Human	Nuclear family (household)	Home territory	Generalized	"the gift"	Band/Egalitarian	Animism
Horticulture/ Pastoral	Human/Animal	Nuclear family (household)/ kinship linkages	Household/ village territory	Generalized Balanced (barter)	"the gift", higher status, other products	Tribes, ranking, development of chiefdoms	Animism/Magic/ Totemism
Agrarian	Human/Animal/ Minimal Machines (water, wind)	Nuclear family (household)/ kinship linkages/ owner of land	Household/ community territory (Cottage Industries)	Generalized, Balanced (barter) between communities, development of negative exchange & a merchant class	"the gift", higher status, other products	Development of states/ stratification	Totemism (ancestor worship) Development of monotheism/ polytheism
Industrial	Machines (non-renewable energy sources)/ Human/Animal	Owners of machines/ factories	Factories, outside of home & community	Negative/ Merchant class controls transport means (profit motive)	Money	States Stratification	Monotheism Polytheism

Adapted from Bonzani. *Bare Backbones: A Brief Introduction to Anthropology.* Cognella, Inc., 2016 (Table 24.1).

Figure 3.2 Example of an early spinning wheel used to spin yarn.
©David Ross/Shutterstock.com

Along comes the steam engine: To see perhaps the last steam engine driven looms working see https://en.wikipedia.org/wiki/File:QSMM_Two_Lancashire_looms.ogv. Developed out of a series of earlier inventions, James Watt then perfects the steam engine to the point where it becomes the "means of production." Individual human labor remains important but the machine and the factory become the loci, location where production occurs.

The factory system changes everything. No longer is production found at the household or community level but it shifts to factories. No longer does the household or kinship group control the means of production and what is produced but that shifts to the "owners" of the means of production, that is, the machine and factory owners, and the way to get to be the owner of a machine or factory is to have capital. In this case capital stands for money.

Also now one does not give their labor as a gift to be repaid in some form at some point in the future (Mauss, 1966 [1925]) nor does one barter what was made in the community for something useful made by another community (a hammock for some corn, for instance) but one gets paid in money and the goal of the transaction is not generalized, balanced, or barter but is negative (Polanyi, 1944; Sahlins, 1972) in the sense that one wants to make a profit off of what they are now exchanging. Here in the factory system we see the three clear indications of capitalism: production and the means of production moves out of the community/village/cottage industry to a factory, the distribution and the means of distribution moves out of the control of the kinship group to an individual, and the goal of the exchange is to make a profit or more money than what the product costs to make.

The requirement of having money or enough capital to invest or build a machine or factory has been identified by Max Weber (1930 [1904–1905, 1920]) as having begun around the time of the Protestant Reformation in Europe in approximately 1517 to 1521. Prior to this time, work did not seem to be, of necessity, in the service of God and many requirements of being a good Catholic met that you gave money to your family members when in need and to the Church, sometimes even having to pay for penitence against your sins. Martin Luther (1517) in his treatise indicates that all believers were of importance in God's eyes and one did not need to go through the clergy or pay penitence to be heard by God. All believers were equal! This new belief changed the face of governments in Europe and eventually around the world and will be discussed further in the next chapter. Here we want to focus on the fact that the Protestant Reformation is believed to have led to the development of capitalism (Weber, 1930 [1904–1905, 1920]): exchange for a profit and private ownership of the means of production by the individual. First, work became a form of service itself to God; the harder and longer one worked the better in the eyes of God. Also one could control their own destiny; to be poor was not preordained by God but that with hard work anyone could succeed; and thirdly, frugal living and savings were promoted so that as an individual you were not expected to give all of your money to the church or your relatives but could accumulate capital. This shift to individual accumulation of capital from status obtained by giving allowed for some individuals to acquire enough money so that they could invest and buy the new means of production which was more and more mechanized and, thus, leading to the globalized capitalistic society that we live in today.

Another example of the use of machines to greatly increase productivity includes in the iron-making industry. When the coal-fire blast furnace is invented, it greatly increases the production of iron. For instance in CE 1788, England produced 68,000 tons of iron and by CE 1845 this had increased 24 times (Braudel, 1981 [1979]). Here if we keep in mind another way to study economic exchanges that focuses on a maximization of returns (Smith, 1776), we see that supply, demand, and price are intimately related. As the demand for a product increases so can its price and its profit to the producer. As more and more people needed and used iron and steel and more and more companies and individuals bought these products, the profits went back to the producing individuals, companies, and countries and these became very wealthy indeed. One needs to only think of Andrew Carnegie and the production of steel in the United States to visualize the vast amounts of money he was able to make as a profit in the sale of this greatly mechanized production of steel.

The Second Phase of the Industrial Revolution

One of the most important developments related to the invention of the steam engine was its use in transportation, leading to large networks of railroads and steamships, starting ca. CE 1850. These large transportation networks led to further contacts between different societies and peoples and led to the opening up of new markets for products now being produced in mass in England and Europe. Again, as products were sold for a profit, this money and capital flowed back to the owners of the means of production and distribution and England, France, the Dutch, Portugal, and other European nations became extremely wealthy and powerful all around the world.

However, as Braudel (1981 [1979]: 102) notes: "It is only a step from market to colony." The Age of Colonialism had come into its own. Colonialism is defined as the political, economic, and cultural domination of a territory and its people by a foreign power for an extended time. It should also be noted that the study of Anthropology also begins at this time to understand the customs and ways of life of these new peoples that Europeans were now encountering. Many problems occur with colonialism and are found in the extractive nature of the encounter. Natural resources and human labor were extracted from these different areas to fund the growing industrial power of "the West" and although slavery has existed in many different human societies at many different times, the trans-Atlantic slave trade geared toward the production of goods for the wealthy and masses and for profit for the European powers is a good example of a terrible consequence of colonialism.

Modern colonialism is noted to have begun before this time in the "Age of Discovery" during which European nations founded colonies throughout the New World (the Americas). An early phase occurred from CE 1492 to 1825 and a more imperialistic phase ran from CE 1850 to just after the end of the Second World War when many states gained independence with many of these territorial units defined by the European powers that once occupied them. Imperialism, by the way, is defined as: "the policy, practice, or advocacy of extending the power and dominion of a nation especially by direct territorial acquisitions or by gaining indirect control over the political or economic life of other areas" (https://www.merriam-webster.com/dictionary/imperialism).

There are numerous important technological innovations that occur at this time. One important one included in the rubber industry with the invention of vulcanization which prevented rubber products from becoming sticky in hot weather. Image trying to drive your car in the summer and having your tires melt on you! Remember at the time there was no synthetic rubber and all rubber had to come from natural rubber trees, mainly from *Hevea brasiliensis* which grew only in Brazil at the time. Another tree that can produce a milky latex sap used as rubber occurs in Central America and is known scientifically as *Castilla elastica*. One of, if not, the earliest evidence of the use of rubber actually comes from an Olmec archaeological site near the Gulf coast of present-day Mexico. The earliest evidence of the actual use of rubber as balls comes from the site El Manatí, located only 10 miles (16 km) southeast of the Olmec site of San Lorenzo and dated ca. BCE 1700 to 1200 (Pool, 2007: 95–98). The site is waterlogged by strong springs and believed to have been used to make offerings to the spirits supplying the spring waters or other supernatural entities. Offerings include wooden busts, polished stone axes, jade and serpentine beads, a wooden staff with a bird's head on one end and a shark's tooth on the other (possibly for blood-letting), and an obsidian knife with an asphalt handle. Skeletons of infants have also been recovered in the offerings.

Going back to the rubber balls, that is why if you ever go to buy tires, one well-known brand is Goodyear and that is who invented or discovered the process of vulcanization in 1844, Charles Goodyear. The name Goodyear Tire & Rubber Company was then used in an American multinational tire manufacturing company founded in 1898 by Frank Seiberling and based in Akron, Ohio.

Other interesting technological innovations in the 1860s include the electric dynamo which allowed for large-scale use of electricity in industries. The transformer was also invented which helped to reduce the loss of energy during its long-distance transmission, all leading to higher efficiency.

Other interesting transformations were occurring in, what we could call the economic section (sector) of industrial societies, that being how businesses were run. Changes were occurring at this time which led to a hierarchy of salaried managers within different businesses. If we go back to our definition of complex societies and recall that a complex society has highly differentiated entities or sections that function to preform different aspects involved in the running of a society, we see that now not only do political, religious, subsistence functions become more specialized and develop hierarchies of individuals but businesses also begin to do this. Big business also becomes institutionalized within a society whereby there are hierarchies of workers whose basic goal is to perform activities directly related to the institution within which they work. Business people in their job functions in essence are not concerned with ethics, are not concerned with medical treatment of sick people, are not concerned with fair wages, etc., but are concerned with the bottom line which as we have seen in industrialized capitalistic societies is making a profit. An interesting documentary called "The Business of America" (California Newsreel, 1984; Feinglass 1984) shows a clip of an interview with the then CEO of U.S. Steel and they ask what is the goal of the business. One would expect perhaps that the CEO would say making high-quality steel but he actually says to make a profit. A profit then appears to be the goal of institutionalized business in the modern industrialized world. In this second phase, business is becoming institutionalized with its own specific functions, hierarchy, and specializations that people learn to do. Here are Merriam-Webster Dictionary's (https://www.merriam-webster.com/dictionary/institution) definition of an institution:

> 1: an act of instituting : ESTABLISHMENT
>
> 2a: a significant practice, relationship, or organization in a society or culture; the *institution* of marriage; something or someone firmly associated with a place or things; he has become an *institution* in the theater
>
> b: an established organization or corporation (such as a bank or university) especially of a public character; financial *institutions*
>
> c: a facility or establishment in which people (such as the sick or needy) live and receive care typically in a confined setting and often without individual consent

I am not sure if these definitions actually help to understand what happens when a society becomes more complex, but this is what we have to work with at this time. This concept and its relationship to the development of big businesses and multinational corporations should be studied more as these entities are often more powerful in today's world then are whole governments of a country and control more wealth and power than do many state governments around the world.

The Third Phase of the Industrial Revolution

Now we move into the early 1900s and into a new phase of the Industrial Revolution. This phase brought in new technologies particularly in the fields of transportation, electricity, and communications. There are many, many inventors that could be cited at this point in the text but for now Thomas Edison who was from Ohio is a good example. He invented the modern light bulb, how to record sound to make phonographs, and early motion pictures. Other important inventions around this time include the internal combustion engine that automobiles use, the telephone, radio, electric generators, and plastics. Here we can ask what is the common denominator in many of these inventions. Most of the time students are unsure of what I am asking for so I go to the next slide in the PowerPoint presentation.

The common denominator in all of these inventions was the focus on the individual. Here now we are beginning to see more and more what Durkheim (1947 [1893]) met when he wrote about societies organized around the division of labor. The division of labor is done at the individual level. The social kinship group becomes less important and it is the individual now that can obtain their own access to resources, not only depend on their position within the family, clan, or house and also not dependent entirely on the position of the kinship group within the larger society within which it exists.

We have entered what some scholars call the "Age of Individualism" (Kottak, 2013: 26–41). These technological innovations allow the individual to: (1) Have access to more resources; (2) Have more decision-making powers on how to spend the money now earned by working outside of the household/village; and (3) Be pulled into the market economy based on the principles of supply, demand, and price/profit, particularly through means of creating the individual's need (demand) for more products. Perhaps here we are already entering the age of consumerism which is tied to the concept of conspicuous consumption whereby goods are consumed not because they are needed but because they add prestige or status to the person within the groups or communities within which they move or live. Sometimes this is also called "keeping up with the Joneses" or the "rat race" where if your neighbor got a new car, then you do also; you cannot use last year's purse to go to the Kentucky Derby even though it is perfectly functional but something is missing, you need to have something new basically to display to your friends and others that you may run into. Thorstein Veblen (1899) noted this in 1899 when he wrote about the leisure classes or the upper classes who had expendable income/money that could be used for display particularly during leisure non—work-related activities like gambling.

The Fourth Phase of the Industrial Revolution

The fourth phase of the Industrial Revolution, which probably should no longer be referred to as a revolution by this time, is sometimes referred to as the "Information Age." These new invented technologies mainly date to after the CE 1950s and have increased the individual's access to information. The main innovations include the television, computers, transistors, the Internet, and different types of plastics. Many of these inventions are debated as to whether they can affect an individual's belief systems. Can television or what someone watches on television or now on a handheld device influence how people think and how they behave? Can contacts over the Internet influence how a person believes or how they act? These questions are debated so I will let the reader do their own research and make up their own minds.

Probably we are still in this fourth phase though I have had students indicate that they think the United States has now moved into a postindustrial stage whereby industry and manufacturing are no longer the major source of income for individuals and are no longer the main drivers of the United States economy. They note that many industries and manufacturing services have moved to other countries that are now industrializing. When we look at the GDP or Gross Domestic Product of different countries, we can track industrial and other sources (service and agricultural are the other two) output through time. GDP is defined as the measure of the value of all of the goods and services produced in a society. Manufacturing is noted to be particularly important because in manufacturing something is created. This product then can be sold on the market and the profit, again, will return to the owners of the means of production and then potentially distributed to workers within the factories or the labor using these mechanical means of production and distribution. If these factories etc., exist in one country, then we should expect the profits to return to the owners, workers, and countries where these products are being produced.

These suppositions of what to expect in a market economy seem to be born out when we look at changes in GDP through time. In 1888, 83 percent of the world's industrial output occurred in five societies: the United States, Britain, Germany, France, and Russia. In 2003, these societies accounted for only 46 percent of the world's industrial output with Japan ranked second (Nolan and Lenski, 2006, 2002). In 2012 the United States, China, Japan, Germany, and France held the highest estimated GDP of any other countries in the world in that order. In 2018, the country ranking based on GDP is similar to 2012 with the United States, China, Japan, Germany, and the United Kingdom listed as the top five countries in that order in terms of the value of all of the goods and services produced in that country (https://countryeconomy.com/gdp). From this brief review of the phases of the Industrial Revolution, we can now go on into the next chapter to identify some of the changes to social, economic, religious, and political aspects of societies that have occurred with industrialization.

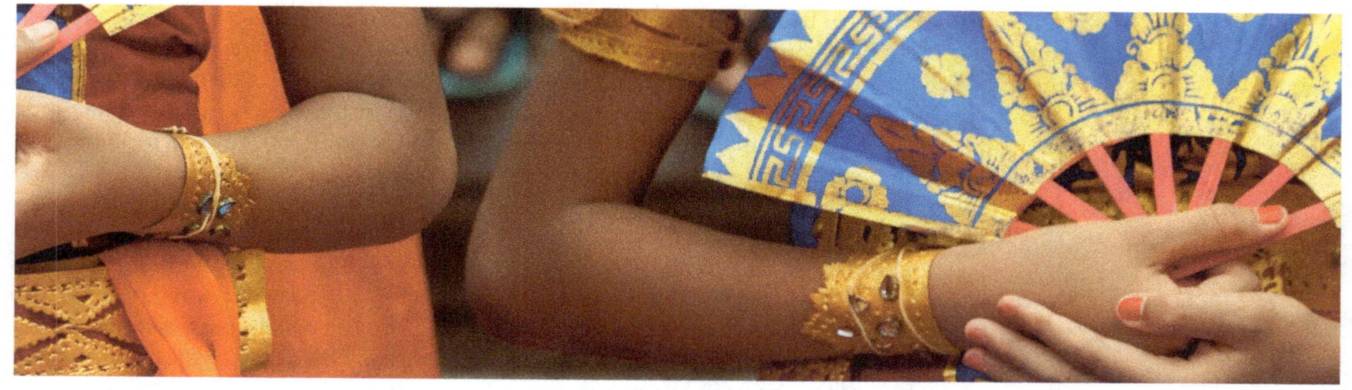

Chapter 4

Industrial Societies

Changing Ideologies, Politics, Marriage and Kinship Practices, and Reproduction Issues

From the previous chapter's brief outline of the phases of the Industrial Revolution, one can begin to notice some changes that have occurred to the sociopolitical and other, such as religious, aspects of societies that are industrialized and that are in the process of industrializing. Again much of this information comes from reading Nolan and Lenski (2006). If one goes back to the fourth phase of the Industrial Revolution and look again at what the focus of many of the inventions and new technologies were, one has to say that they are geared toward the individual. These are inventions that allow individual access to, in particular, communication, as well as travel. These inventions made access more available and indeed more efficient.

This focus on the individual or the Age of Individualism or the continued importance of the individual can be briefly discussed in terms of four major differences that can be identified in industrial societies when compared to nonindustrial societies. These include:

1. Breakdown of kinship structures.
2. Development of private property versus communal property.
3. Stress of the individual in religious ideologies.
4. Stress of the individual in political and secular ideologies.

Breakdown of Kinship Structures

As indicated in the previous chapter, the breakdown in kinship structures, such as the importance of the clan, can partially be traced to economic changes that occurred when the location for the production of useful goods shifted from the household and village or community which involved mainly family members to a location that was controlled outside of the family or clan or house. This can probably be traced back to the invention of a factory system where people, to work or produce, moved outside of their houses or family lands to an area controlled by nonrelated people. This movement allowed for individuals to work on their own and become the "Bosses" of their own income and resources. One did not have to depend on the family anymore. The typical kinship structure indicating this type of economic interaction is the nuclear family. The nuclear family and its individuals become more important and larger kinship networks that traced ties further back in time were less important or "broke down."

Neolocal residence patterns and the nuclear family are typical kinship and marriage residence patterns seen in industrial societies like the United States. Many of us individuals here in the United States leave home, often to go to college, and then get jobs far from home. We make our own money and can spend it as we decide. Maybe we send some back home, if need be or if possible, but this is not mandatory or expected. On the other hand, when we leave home Mom and Dad or one or the other probably do not expect to have to support us by sending money for our food and rent, cars, and cell phones.

Development of Private Property versus Communal Property

Point number two is also obviously economic in its interactions and impact. The rise of capitalism, again defined as the private or individual ownership of the means of production and distribution, also seems to be very much related to this shift in terms of where things are produced and who controls the means of production (i.e., land, machines like tractors, sewing machines, trucks, etc.). An individual who has had the capital to develop or invest now owns the factory and the machines to make the product. This is part of capitalism: The individual is the owner (controls) the means of production and distribution. The other aspect is that the form of payment is no longer in useful goods but is in a medium of exchange accepted to have a similar value by the parties involved, often nonrelatives, and it could be members of different ethnic groups and religions who are involved. This is termed money. However, the form of exchange is referred to as negative exchange (Polyani, 1944; Sahlins, 1972, 1968). In negative exchange systems, the goal of the exchange is to make a profit, that is, more money than it costs to produce the product.

The other reciprocal exchange systems include generalized exchange, sometimes referred to as "the gift" (Mauss, 1966[1925]), whereby the return of the exchange is not immediate and the exchange value is not stipulated. Here the act and development of reciprocity is important: a gift is given (money, food, labor, etc.); it is accepted by the receiver; and in the future it is expected that the gift will be returned to the giver by the receiver. The other reciprocal exchange system is referred to as balanced exchange or one could image barter. Here useful products to both individuals and groups are exchanged. In capitalism and with private property, the individual owns the property and the goal of exchange is for a profit. However, you can find all three types of exchanges in capitalistic societies like in the United States.

Stress of the Individual in Religious Ideologies

For point number three, if one looks at a time scale it is clear to see that all of the world's major religions including Christianity, Islam, Judaism, Buddhism, Hinduism, and others were founded in the agrarian era long before industrialization and its concomitant changes to kinship structures and economic relations occurred. Agrarian refers to the intensive use of land (waterways can also be intensively utilized for food) to produce large amounts of food for large amounts of people, some of which are not the food producers themselves. The agrarian era is when many of the great civilizations of the world arose by producing surpluses to support hierarchically developing political/religious systems (Diamond, 2005). One can, therefore, see that some of the founding principles of these religions might be out of sync with modern or today's reality of life. Nolan and Lenski (2006) point out a few basic differences between the practices of societies and ethnic groups who follow their respective traditional religions and those groups of people who live in more industrialized societies.

Indeed, some followers of traditional religions, whatever that religion might be, are often referred to as Fundamentalists. After conferring with other professors and students, the use of this term seems to be identifying individuals of a particular religion, sometimes also called a religious sect, that would like to return to the fundamental teachings of their religion, as found in the original texts or as fostered by the original founders or prophets. The main problem with this goal or desire does not seem to be so much that people want to return to a simpler way of living with high morals, for instance, but that they want to return to an era that was very different from what it is today: an era when there were no machines and no need to feed seven billion people, an era when in many places individual families or kinship groups controlled the land on which they were able to get their food. Those days are long gone as many of us live in cities, own basically nothing, and especially do not own any land to produce our own food; and, if we did, how would we store it over the winter without mechanized refrigeration or factories that make can goods. This is just one of a myriad of other examples to show how difficult it would be to get back to the fundamental lifestyles promoted in many religious texts that can be over 1,500 years old now.

So…. What are some of the differences between the beliefs or lifestyles of religious groups of people living in traditional nonindustrial contexts and those peoples, many who are also very religious, that live in an industrialized world and have done so for about 250 or more years now. Five examples of some differences can easily come to mind. However, before that, one needs to review very briefly how the individual has become more important in at least one of these major religions.

In Christianity and particularly in the Christian denomination of Catholicism, one can, of course, pray to God but to be forgiven of sins the masses need to go through the Priest. One has to go to Confession with a Priest and then the Priest will tell you some things to do and prayers to recite to be forgiven for the sins committed. The individual access to God is channeled through a hierarchy as one would expect in complex societies with institutionalized religious structures. In the early 1500s, however, a priest by the name of Martin Luther wrote about changing this. In particular, he disagreed with religious members having to pay a sum or fee to the Catholic Church to have their sins absolved (this practice being referred to as indulgences). This change in perspective is referred to as the Protestant Reformation and in these teachings the individual becomes more important.

First, the individual himself or herself could communicate directly with God. As Nolan and Lenski (2006: 244) write: "The Protestant doctrine of the priesthood of all believers - the doctrine that all believers are equal in God's sight and can relate directly to Him without the mediation of the clergy." The individual then is a viable force in the interpretation of the Bible and could control his or her own destiny without the mediation of the clergy. Also these teachings changed the way people viewed work in that work itself became a form of service to God and the individual himself or herself could accumulate capital or money in this process. The need to pay for church services or to sponsor church festivities for the larger community seems to have been undercut: The accumulation of private money and private property was not a sin but revealed one's honoring God by their hard work.

Very importantly for political reasons, one sees that all believers, all individuals, are equal in God's eyes. This aspect can be interpreted as meaning that no individuals or family lines are preordained by God as being more important or destined to be the king or the queen of a land. This aspect of the equality of all individuals is the backbone to the political structure of democracies. These views take hundreds of years to take hold but the French Revolution in 1799 and the Russian Revolution in 1917 (let alone the "American Revolution" beginning in 1776) are examples of overthrowing monarchies that had been based on the concept that these noble families were different or preordained by God to be in their positions of power. This concept does not work in a democracy.

Further as identified by Max Weber (1930 [1904–1905, 1920] in his work called "The Protestant Ethic and the Spirit of Capitalism," this shift in religious ideologies toward the importance of the individual is seen as a major shift toward capitalism. Basically, it seems that three aspects of work change. First as mentioned, work itself was an important service to God. It was important to work as hard as possible and this would lead to rewards that could occur while one was alive. Many people have heard of the "Protestant work ethic" which means that if one has that, one is a hard worker! And it is alright or even a goal to save the money earned while working.

Secondly, these Protestant faiths undermine the concept of fatalism and spreads, more so, the ideas that individuals have control over what happens to them. This view also undermines a belief in magic which can be defined as "the use of means (such as charms or spells) believed to have supernatural power over natural forces" (https://www.merriam-webster.com/dictionary/magic) or the use of fetishes, potions, etc. to influence supernatural entities to make something happen in the future that one wants to happen (both good and bad outcomes or positive and negative outcomes). Instead, rationalism or "a belief or theory that opinions and actions should be based on reason and knowledge rather than on religious belief or emotional response" (https://www.google.com/search?q=definition+rationalim&rlz=1C1CHFX_enUS705US705&oq=definition+rationalim&aqs=chrome..69i57j0l5.4385j1j7&sourceid=chrome&ie=UTF-8) becomes more widespread. Finally, with work people began to be able to accumulate capital or money. One cannot build a machine or make a factory without the capital investment. This ability of the individual and not the family to invest in "industry" led, then, to capitalism, which is again, the individual's control or ownership of the means of production and distribution. These are all changes that have been traced back to the beginnings of the Protestant Reformation and the growing importance of the individual.

Returning to Fundamentalist religious sects, individuals in these sects seem to reject most of the values upon which economic growth and development in the modern (today's) world occur. These differences in values lead to conflicts between an individualistic view of the world and a view of the world based on the agrarian faiths. There are certainly more but five examples can be cited of this.

Education

In some traditionally religious societies, education is limited to the religious texts and is generally not available to the masses of people. Often this education is actually limited to males. In industrial individualistic societies, education is often public and the intent is for all children, both males and females to attend. Furthermore, the curricula are based on reading, writing, and arithmetic with some religious texts covered in private religious schools. More so, the focus on STEM (science, technology, engineering, and math) courses and curricula that one sees in schools in many industrial and industrializing countries like the United States is understandable if one of the goals of the education is for the invention and innovation of technologies which can lead to "modernization" or "development." To develop new technologies, one can be religious, but one also must have a foundation in science-based curricula. A big gap in technologies and "modernization" between these different types of societies just based on educational training can clearly develop through time.

The Afterlife

In many traditional religions true fulfillment comes after death. An acceptance of the conditions of the world can be stressed and even the religion can promote subservience in this life as things will get better in the next. In industrial societies, the majority of people have little patience for unacceptable conditions such as bad sanitation, as one of many examples. Particularly in societies where taxes are collected to improve conditions now and not after one is dead, people will often go to town meetings or become members of civil—civic organizations to promote for the improvement of their communities.

Governments

In many traditional religious societies, the goal is to have the political system run by the religious leaders. These types of political systems have been decreasing through time as more and more state-level societies lean toward becoming democracies (see Figure 2.1). Such political systems can be termed theocracies, or governments run by the religious leaders, and monarchies which are governments run by noble family lines based on hereditary kings and queens whose powers were seen to be vested in God. In democracies as stated previously, individual rights and freedoms are the foundation of democracies, thereby, negating the view that anyone has been vested a priori with powers giving them the divine right to rule. Hereditary rule does not work in a democracy. Political leaders must be elected and, theoretically, their election should be based on achieved status and power and not ascribed or inherited status and power. More on this to follow shortly.

Figure 4.1 Total Fertility Rates of the World from 1990 to 2000.

Key: Adapted from: Allen, John L., and Audrey C. Shalinsky. *Student Atlas of Anthropology*. New York: McGraw-Hill Companies, 2004.

Map: ©dikobraziy/Shutterstock.com

Birth control

The debate about the use of birth control seems to be growing and this section does not address abortion; here, we are talking about birth control used to stop a pregnancy before it happens, like condoms, the pill, the morning-after pill, IUDs...if you are female or for that matter, male, in the United States and reading this, you should know what I mean.

Remember the major world religions all first arose in preindustrial societies; many of which required large families to be able to work the land or move the animals. In some locations around the world and even within the United States with traditional lifestyles, types of societies and communities, this still occurs and large families are great but in industrial societies with billions of people who have no access to land and often live in one or less bedroom apartments in big skyscrapers, large families are a thing of the past.

How do you control births and birth rates? Birth control. In general, in industrial societies like the United States, birth control is legal. You can go to the corner grocery store or pharmacy and buy birth control over the counter. Why does this matter or work that way? What difference does it make if a woman has one, two, three, four, five, or more children? One way to look at it is over time. As illustrated in Figure 4.1, women in industrial societies have a 1.6 total fertility rate (TFR). This rate is lower than women who live in nonindustrial societies who average a TFR of 3.1 (TFR is an estimate of the number of children the average woman will have in her lifetime).

Visualize an upside-down pyramid representing birth rates over time of four women: two in an industrial society and two in a nonindustrial society using the TFRs given above (Figure 4.2):

By the third generation in a society where let's say each woman has two children in her lifetime, there will be sixteen children. If the family or household has $10,000 to spend on these third generation children, then each child has access to $625. Let's say in a nonindustrial society each woman has three children, then by the third generation that equals fifty-four children. Here one can easily see how one additional child per women can quickly add up to a lot of children to take care of and how with the same $10,000 income, one could end up in poverty trying to take care of fifty-four children with only being able to spend $185.19 per child. The same $10,000 income in both locations has to be used to take care of fifty-four children in one place and sixteen in another. That might be why when I visited the Department of Amazonas in Colombia and the women I met each had on average ten children, one of the first things they asked me about was birth control. Now if the family controls the land, has access to resources and can produce their own food, these large families may not be a problem but what about in an industrial city. Try to send even two children to college, which is very necessary now in industrial societies for them make a good salary, with the tuition costs at the level that they are today ("According to the College Board, the average cost of tuition and fees for the 2017–2018 school year was $34,740 at private colleges, $9,970 for state residents at public colleges, and $25,620 for out-of-state residents attending public universities" [https://www.collegedata.com/en/pay-your-way/college-sticker-shock/how-much-does-college-cost/whats-the-price-tag-for-a-college-education/]). In this scenario one can begin to see why birth control in a modern world could be necessary.

Per Capita (Individual) $ Availability of $10,000	**$10000/16 = $625**	**$10000/54 = $185.19**
Children third generation	1 1 1 1 1 1 1 1 1 1 1 1 1 1 1 1	1 1 1 1 1 1 1 1 1 1 1 1 1 1 1 1 1 1 1 1 1 1 1 1 1 1 1 1 1 1 1 1 1 1 1 1 1 1 1 1 1 1 1 1 1 1 1 1 1 1 1 1 1 1
Children second generation	1 1 1 1 1 1 1 1	1 1 1 1 1 1 1 1 1 1 1 1 1 1 1 1 1 1
Children first generation	1 1 1 1	1 1 1 1 1 1
Number of women	1 1	1 1
	Industrial Country	Non-industrial Country
	TFR = 1.6	TFR = 3.1

Figure 4.2 Hypothetical Effects of TFR in Industrial and Nonindustrial Countries.

Tolerance

Peoples who are very fundamental about their religious beliefs in general seem to be very intolerant of people who are different from them. In fact sometimes these different people are not considered to be human or will be punished by God for the fact of not believing and following the teachings of the prophet or founder of the major agrarian religion which the other person believes in. In industrial societies, people tend to be more tolerant because for one reason, they generally have interactions with people of different families, religions, political stance on a daily basis and this often occurs at work or at the schools that their children attend. Remember one is no longer just working in a village or household or with all their family members or even with people who speak the same language. One can be working with someone from a different part of the world in the office or even through the internet. It is always a good idea to try to get along with your coworkers even if they are not your family members or part of the same ethnic group as you are.

Stress of the Individual in Political and Secular Ideologies

Finally, number four is where one can see a stress of the individual in secular ideologies and politics. There are many secular ideologies. First of all, what does secular mean? (Aiyar, 2008). Secular is defined by Merriam-Webster as follows (https://www.merriam-webster.com/dictionary/secular):

> **1:** of or relating to the worldly or temporal *secular* concerns
>
> **b:** not overtly or specifically religious *secular* music
>
> **c:** not ecclesiastical or clerical *secular* courts *secular* landowners
>
> **2:** not bound by monastic vows or rules *specifically*: of, relating to, or forming clergy not belonging to a religious order or congregation a *secular* priest
>
> **3a:** occurring once in an age or a century
>
> **b:** existing or continuing through ages or centuries
>
> **c:** of or relating to a long term of indefinite duration *secular* inflation

Basically, the definition indicates that secular means beliefs and practices that are not religious in nature. There are many of these ideologies including capitalism, democratic republicanism, oligarchical republicanism, socialism, democratic socialism, revolutionary socialism (communism), nationalism, pragmatism, and hedonism.

As noted, in many countries of the world a trend toward democracies seems to be occurring (Figure 2.1). Democracy can be defined as a form of government in which the supreme power is retained by the people collectively and the peoples' power is exercised directly or indirectly through the electoral process. It does not always work but the important aspect is: "the exercise of the powers of government to benefit the masses of ordinary people in countless ways" (Nolan and Lenski, 2006: 242). One problem can occur with plutocracies which are governments run by the rich. The problem can be seen in the fact that rich people do not deal with the same problems as do less rich or poor people. Probably most rich people do not have to worry about if they will have enough money from their job to have food for the whole month. Nor do they probably worry about if they get sick and do not have insurance or have money to send their children to college. These differences in lifestyles and concerns might not give them the perspectives needed to represent the majority of people in a society and especially in highly hierarchical societies where there is a big gap between the rich and the poor.

What might be some causes of the increase in democracies around the world? First, the Protestant Reformation and the spread of Christianity and Protestantism, in particular, has led to a belief in the equality of all peoples. One can see this clearly in the United States Declaration of Independence (1776) whereby: "We hold these truths to be self-evident, that all men are created equal, that they are endowed by their Creator with certain unalienable Rights, that among these are Life, Liberty, and the pursuit of Happiness" (http://archives.gov/exhibits/charters/declaration_transcript.html).

Further, the conquest of the New World opened up lands for the development of governments which were not burdened by rulers that had already inherited their statuses. For a general review of the dire consequences to native peoples of these conquests and colonization in the New World see Denevan (1976), Diamond (2005), and Hemming (1978a, 1978b, 1987). These new colonizers could break away from the already institutionalized form of monarchy found in most of Europe at the time. Try to establish a new government when the kings' soldiers come to knock at the door.

Finally, industrialized societies require a high level of education to be able to create and run these new and old technologies. Education allows people to intelligently question authority and as everyone knows: "Knowledge is Power." From just this brief review of the Industrial Revolution and characteristics of industrial societies, one can see that these societies and people can be very different from nonindustrial or more traditional societies around the world that are still based on a kinship access to status, power, and wealth.

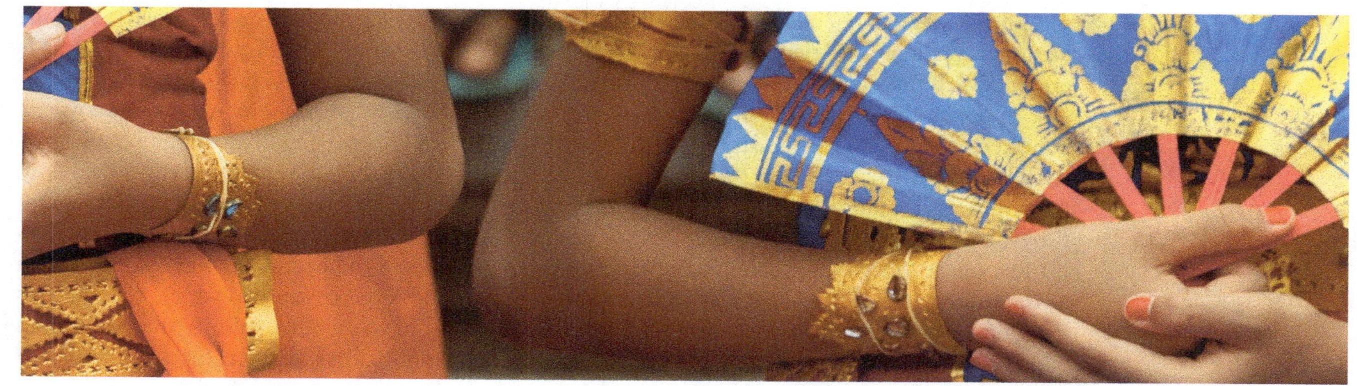

Chapter 5

Case Study on Marriage and Descent Practices

The League of the Iroquois

For this chapter an outline of the kinship structures of an indigenous group, the League of the Iroquois, is given to supply an example of how kinship works in a traditional nonindustrial society. To do this I tried to choose an indigenous group from what is now part of the United States of America and Canada that has different subsistence strategies to get food, different religious beliefs, and a different political system than what most citizens of the United States are familiar with today. I also wanted a society that was different from what most U.S. citizens and students had experiences with, in terms of how they trace descent, what they call their relatives, and what their marriage patterns are, as these terms were defined in previous chapters.

The structure of this chapter is based off of the book by Janice E. Stockard "Marriage in Culture" (2002) which I have used numerous times in lectures on marriage patterns and which I felt was well written and easy to understand for me and for the students. For the Iroquois, an original older ethnography by Lewis Henry Morgan (1962 [1851]) was utilized to gain an insight into their kinship patterns and other aspects of their society and this information is referenced below throughout the text. It should be noted that Morgan's use of the term "nations" is now interpreted to mean "tribe" in anthropological terms and his use of the term "tribe" to describe the kinship subdivisions within each nation is interpreted to mean "clan" in anthropological terms (Stockard, 2002: 58–80). I have basically kept the original terminology as found in Morgan (1962 [1851]) for this chapter. Definitions and further discussions of these terms occur in Chapter 7.

League of the Iroquois

The information for this section of the chapter comes from Lewis Henry Morgan's pioneer ethnography entitled "League of the *Ho-de-no-sau-nee*, or Iroquois" (1851 with the 1962 edition utilized herein). Lewis Henry Morgan was born near Aurora on Cayuga Lake in the state of New York in 1818. He made a fortune as a corporate lawyer in Rochester and speculated on railroads and mining in upper Michigan. He also represented Rochester in the State Legislature and was elected to the National Academy of Sciences in 1875. He is known as the Father of U.S. Anthropology and he is credited with this work as giving birth to American ethnology (Morgan, 1962: IX; Resek, 1960).

Importantly and by chance, Morgan met a young interpreter *Ha-sa-no-an-da*, who was a Seneca on his way to sachemship (chiefdomship), while he was browsing in an Albany bookstore. Also known as Ely S. Parker, this young man was an unusual individual who felt comfortable in two cultures. He later became a civil engineer, future aide-de-camp of General U.S. Grant, and at times the Commissioner of Indian Affairs. He gave Morgan access to the tribes of the Iroquois Nation where Morgan was able to conduct numerous interviews and he helped him compile much of the information in this book as well as the classificatory system of kinship which Morgan was to build into his monumental work on "Systems of Consanguinity and Affinity of the Human Family" (1871). Morgan also began early studies in sociopolitical systems in his work "Ancient Society" (1877).

For about a century from 1600 to 1700, the Iroquois are noted to have been in constant warfare. They subdued numerous indigenous groups in the territories now found in the states of New York, Delaware, Maryland, New Jersey, Pennsylvania, northern and western Virginia, Ohio, Kentucky, northern Tennessee, Illinois, Indiana, Michigan, a part of the New England States and a principal part of Upper Canada (Morgan 1962 [1851]: 14–15). During the same period from about 1640 to 1700, constant warfare occurred between the French and the Iroquois. A general peaceful time ensued until the war of 1755 which led to the conquest of the French by the English in 1766 (Morgan 1962 [1851]: 21–22).

Around 1650 before their encounters with the Europeans, the league was at its greatest prosperity and height (Figure 5.1). Their total population could easily be placed at 25,000 if not more. The League at that time was comprised of five nations or what today are referred to as tribes (Stockard, 2002: 69) and included the Senecas (10,000 in population), the Cayugas (3,000), the Onondagas (4,000), the Oneidas (3,000), and the Mohawks (5,000). A century later their total population was estimated at only half of this number. In 1715, the Tuscaroras, who were expelled from North Carolina, moved north to seek refuge in Iroquois territory. After this event, the Iroquois who had been referred to by the English as the "Five Nations" became known under the name of the "Six Nations" (Morgan 1962 [1851]: 24–27).

From the end of the French War until the American Revolution, times seem to have been more peaceful. During the Revolution they were basically neutral until finally they joined England as a "transatlantic ally." Not all of the nations of the Iroquois agreed with this and in a weakened position each nation determined if it might engage in war with the Mohawks, Onondagas, Cayugas, and Senecas taking up arms with the English. In the treaty of peace between Great Britain and the United States in 1783, no provisions were made for the Iroquois who were abandoned by the English allies and left to make their own terms with the new federation. Finally, the jurisdiction of the United States extended over their ancient territories and thenceforth they became dependent nations under the United States of America (Morgan 1962 [1851]: 27–28).

The territory this League of Nations controlled was indeed large and its political configuration is considered a confederacy as it was comprised of six nations that were essentially considered equal in political influence and autonomy. For the Iroquois a fundamental law was unanimity in decision making. If one of the nations disagreed with a course of action, the motion was defeated. A confederation is defined as: "When a group of people or nations form an alliance, it is called a confederation, allowing each member to govern itself but agreeing to work together for common causes" (https://www.vocabulary.com/dictionary/confederation).

This confederation, one could argue, was similar to a complex state. It was divided into administrative units based on the nation and each nation was assigned particular duties and rights. Basic parts of a definition of a state, to follow in succeeding chapters, are that it has a centralization of power and the legitimate control and use of violence. This confederation had both. Although each nation was politically autonomous, the Onondagas were given the hereditary grant of the "Council Brand" and also of the "Wampum" into which the laws of the League "had been talked." The council-fire in the Onondaga valley was in effect the seat of government (Morgan 1962 [1851]: 94). Here we see a centralized place of decision making and power and a form of recording.

Figure 5.1 Location of the League of the Iroquois in the 1600s to 1700s.

Although not a written language, the wampum conveyed knowledge and were woven strings and belts of leather and sinew strung with spiral freshwater shells, *Ote-ko'-ã* (Figure 5.2). There were white and purple types with white beads made out of the inside of the great conch shell and the purple worked out of the inside of the muscle shell. These belts were as wide as a hand and two feet long and were given and received as treaties of agreements and friendship. They operated on a principle of association and memory and were mnemonic devices of power (Morgan 1962 [1851]: 120–121).

In terms of a standing military and the legitimate use of violence, the Senecas were noted to have been awarded the two highest military chieftains. This may have been done since the Seneca controlled the western boundaries of the League from which hostile attacks were to be expected and

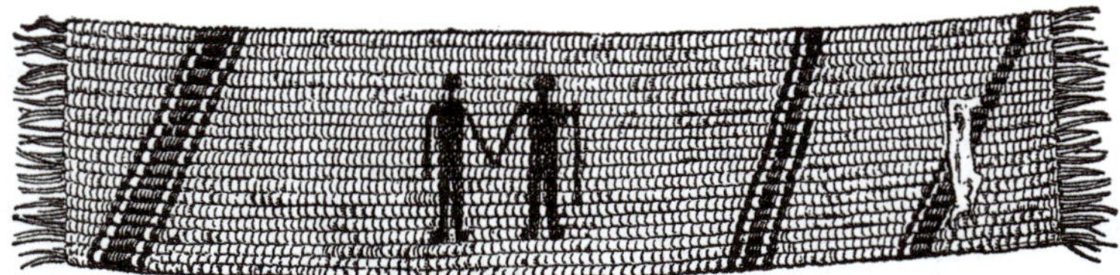

Figure 5.2 Example of Wampum, a Means of Association and Mnemonic Devices of Power Utilized by the Iroquois.
©Morphart Creation/Shutterstock.com

indeed the construction of their long houses ("their political edifice, the Long House") with the door opening to the west was noted by Morgan (1962 [1851]: 94–95) to have been done for that reason as well. The Mohawks were noted to be the hereditary receivers of tribute. These are hereditary positions as are found in chiefdoms and ancient state complex societies.

However, there are some characteristics of ancient states that appear to be missing from the League of the Iroquois. One difference is that in ancient states and empires the central ruling family will often trace descent to an all mighty Creator God. The Iroquois are known to have a belief in the Great Spirit, credited with being the creator, ruler, and preserver of life. Although "the earth grew miraculously on its own," the Great Spirit created animals, the vegetable world, and "adapted the elements, and the whole visible universe to the wants of man" (Morgan 1962 [1851]: 154). They also had a belief in what in Anthropology is called animism or a belief in an "invisible world with spiritual existences" (Morgan 1962 [1851]: 151). However, none of these beliefs seems to have developed into a hereditary ruling family linked by kinship ties to the Great Spirit. Instead although each nation had inherited special privileges that all would abide by, the fact remained that each nation was independent and each had equal participation and veto rights in the administration of the government.

The nations, themselves, were divided into two classes or divisions and when assembled were arranged on opposite sides of the "council-fire." On one side were the Mohawks, Onondagas, and Senecas that were regarded as "brothers" to each and "fathers" to the other nations. On the other side were the Oneidas and Cayugas and the Tuscaroras, who were brother nations and children to the first three.

What was the Iroquois Nations' descent system like? Herein we will see that the terms and concepts covered in previous chapters will come in handy. These terms include moiety, exogamy, matrilineal descent, arranged marriages, monogamy, and matrilocal residence patterns. Morgan (1962 [1851]: 82–84) states that in effect this League of Nations was a "League of Tribes." Each of the nations was divided into eight of what he refers to as tribes (although in a footnote he notes that the Senecas had eight tribes, the Cayugas eight, the Tuscaroras seven, the Onondagas eight, the Oneidas three, and the Mohawks three). Stockard (2002: 69) explains that these tribes are actually what in Anthropology today are referred to as clans (see definition below).

Some of these were exogamous, meaning that they could not intermarry within themselves (see Morgan 1962 [1851]: 80 for the Seneca and scientific names of these tribes). These were the Wolf, Bear, Beaver, and Turtle tribes that were considered brothers to each other and could not intermarry. The four opposite tribes were also considered brothers and could not intermarry. These were the Deer, Snipe, Heron, and Hawk with tradition declaring that the Bear and Deer were the original tribes. The first four tribes could marry the second four tribes since they were considered cousins and not brothers. Here we see exogamy which seems to be reinforcing a duality or a moiety system in which all of the nations and the tribes (clans) at a lower level are broken into two segments and the necessity to marry out of the group weaves them together through time (see Figure 7.2).

Further, we see that all of the relatives of the father laterally or collaterally in his generation and all of the relatives of the mother laterally or collaterally in her generation are brothers and sisters or fathers and mothers to the children of the father and his brothers and the mother and her sisters. In Anthropology this is referred to as bifurcate merging kinship terminology that is associated to unilineal descent groups, either patrilineal or matrilineal, with patrilocal or matrilocal marriage residence patterns and often found in horticultural, pastoral, and agricultural societies.

This association of brothers and sisters was likewise applied to anyone of the same tribe (clan) even if from a different nation (tribe). This system created ties of brotherhood that linked the nations together with indissoluble bonds. For instance, when the Mohawk of the Wolf tribe recognized and greeted the Seneca of the Wolf tribe, they did so as brothers; they felt bound to each other through ties of consanguinity (blood ties). Morgan actually seems to credit this for the strength of the League of the Iroquois when he writes (1962 [1851]: 81: "It became the means of effecting the most perfect union of separate nations 'ever devised by the wit of man.'") Again, he indicates this because although an individual belonged to a particular nation, that is, the Seneca, and would have had very strong lineal or descent ties to the tribe and nation, when he ran into a member of his same tribe, that is, Deer, even from another nation, they were "brothers." They felt that union of kinship that calms or quenches internal disputes and unifies peoples.

Importantly, one could be many generations from a founding father but still be a brother to someone who otherwise one might consider as a very distant third, fourth, or fifth cousin or perhaps not even related at all in a differently configured kinship system! This collateral ability to unify members of different kinship groups like clans or tribes, may also help to explain the fluid nature of these entities (tribes) as described by Evans-Pritchard (1940) whereby they can be comprised of separate autonomous units yet under threat of attack can coalesce as sibs or "sibling" into large daunting warrior parties (also see Smith, 2006; see https://www.etymonline.com/word/sibling: Old English *sibling* "relative, kinsman," from *sibb*" kinship, relationship; love, friendship, peace, happiness," from Proto-Germanic **sibja-*"blood relation, relative," properly "one's own"). Fox (1967: 167–168) explains that sibs are not descent units or even groups of people, but are categories of people out of which a group can be recruited by ego for some purpose (i.e., for military protection or to make payments of blood money to the kindred of a man killed by ego). These transitory entities are also referred to as segmentary clan and lineage systems (Cole 1975: 82, 91–93).

In some sense then these tribes seem to be equivalent to clans (Stockard, 2002: 69) who trace membership back to an apical ancestor who is not known but is often represented or associated to a totem. The totem is usually an animal or plant used to represent the group and the ancestors whose spirits continue to live on and affect the members of the clan or totem. In Anthropology this is referred to as totemism or a cult to the ancestors. The Iroquois and other Native American groups are known to have had seasonal dances associated to specific animal or plant spirit entities. The dancers were often masked in representation of the totem spirits who controlled and affected the seasonal abundance and availability of food sources and their continued productivity and reciprocity in relation to the human group (Morgan, 1962 [1851]: 182–225; also see Oyuela-Caycedo, 2004; Oyuela-Caycedo and Fischer, 2006).

How was descent actually traced? The Iroquois are interesting to many Anthropologists and others because they are matrilineal: Descent is traced through the mother while in many societies today that practice unilineal descent, descent is traced through the male line. For instance, Stockard (2002: 60) estimates that only 15 percent of the world's cultures practice matrilineal descent and these are horticultural societies and rarely agrarian, pastoral, industrial, or postindustrial societies (also see Schneider and Gough 1961). Basically, in a matrilineal society transmission of all titles, rights, and property runs in the female line to the exclusion of the male. When a man and woman married, as noted, they had to be of different tribes (clans) and moieties. However, the children always belonged to the mother's tribe (clan).

This does not mean that men, brothers, and sons did not have power. Indeed, a male could hold a sachemship (chieftainship) but the descent of the title was limited to the female line. It could not pass out of the tribe of the mother. The mother inherited this right through her mother who had inherited it through her mother and so on. Her son could then hold the title of sachem but the son of her brother, who belonged to his own mother's tribe and not his father's tribe, could not.

Morgan (1962 [1851]: 84) notes that the inheritance of a man and the sachemship could go to his brothers, or his sister's children, or even under some circumstances to some individual of the tribe at large, each of whom were in his tribe; while his children, being of another tribe, were placed out of the line of succession. The rule of descent for the child was that the child must be the son of its mother, although not necessarily of its mother's husband.

"To understand this subject, it must be borne in mind, that of the grandparents one only, the maternal grandmother, necessarily was, and of the parents only the mother, and, in descending line, only the sisters' children could be of the same tribe with the propositus, or individual from whom the degrees of relationship reckoned… The maternal grandmother and her sisters were equally grandmothers; the mother and her sisters were equally mothers; the children of a mother's sisters were considered brothers and sisters; the children of a sister were nephews and nieces; and the grandchildren of a sister were his grandchildren. These were the chief relatives within the tribe, though not fully extended as to number. Out of the tribe, the paternal grandfather and his brothers were equally grandfathers; the father and his brothers equally fathers; the father's sisters were aunts, while in the tribe, the mother's brothers were uncles; the father's sister's children were cousins, as in civil law; the children of these cousins were nephews and nieces; and the children of these nieces and nephews were his grandchildren, or the children of his propositus. Again, the children of his brother were his children, and the grandchildren of a brother were his grandchildren; also, the children of a father's brother were his brothers and sisters, instead of cousins, as under civil law; and lastly, their children were his grandchildren" (Morgan 1962 [1851]: 85–86, for the names in the language of the Seneca see pg. 86).

Here we see the collateral or lateral line merged into the lineal line of descent and none of the collaterals (or to us distant cousins) were lost by remoteness of degree (see Figures 2.7 and 7.2). Collateral relatives are in essence horizontal layers of kin; they are the siblings of the core nuclear family members and the children of ego's own siblings (Fox, 1967: 259). Put another way, collateral relatives are "relatives that are neither direct ancestors nor direct descendants of an individual (e.g., siblings, aunts, uncles, nieces, and nephews)" (http://groups.molbiosci.northwestern.edu/holmgren/Glossary/Definitions/Def-C/collateral_relatives.html) (I envision this like the structure of the long house or bark house with the upright poles representing the lineal descent lines and the cross poles representing the collateral and fictive relations of brothers and sisters of clans and tribes that held the Iroquois Nation together).

The title of sachem was absolutely hereditary within the tribe to which it was assigned, but there was no law of primogeniture whereby the first born son would inherit the title, rights, or land; there appears to have been no law or preference between children based on order of birth (Morgan, 1962 [1851]: 87). These positions (i.e., sachem or chief) can be considered to be ascribed whereby one is born into a particular position. Between the male members of the tribe itself a title was elective. Upon the death of a sachem, a tribal council assembled to determine the successor. The choice was usually one of the deceased sister's sons or one of his brothers. An infant could be named with only the necessity of setting up a guardian until he attained a suitable age. If on misconduct, a sachem lost the confidence or trust and respect of his tribe and was deemed unworthy of authority, a tribal council at once deposed him. Naming of a child also strongly reflected the tribe to which the child belonged and after the birth at the next council meeting the birth and name were announced as were the names of the tribes of the father and the mother (Morgan, 1962 [1851]:88–89).

Marriages were arranged and monogamous. It appears to have been a contract between mothers acting in consultation with the matrons and wisemen of the tribes concerned. Emotional attachment between the two people to be wed is indicated to have not been important. In older times a young warrior would be married to a woman several years his senior. The time of marriage indicated to be twenty-five so he could "become inured to the hardships of the war path and of the chase, before his freedom was curtailed and his responsibilities were increased in the cares of a family…" (Morgan, 1962 [1851]: 320). The women could often be a widow and widowers at sixty could be joined to a woman at twenty, but it is noted that in more recent times the ages of the parties drew nearer to being the same and the marriage age was reduced in time to twenty or even below that. The parties were often completely ignorant of these negotiations perhaps only being aware of this at the announcement of their marriage. Apparently, not much complaining occurred and "they received each other as the gift of their parents" (Morgan, 1962 [1851]: 321).

After the marriage announcement, a simple ceremony followed. On the day after the announcement, the woman was conducted by her mother and a few female friends to the home of her intended husband. She carried in her hands a few cakes of unleavened corn bread. She presented these to her mother-in-law upon entering the house as an indication of her earnestness and skill in the domestic domain. After receiving this, the mother of the young man returned a gift of venison or other game

Figure 5.3 Illustration of a Long House of the Historic Iroquois.

animal to the mother of the bride as an indication of his earnestness and ability to provide for the family. This exchange of gifts ratified and concluded the contract of marriage which bound the two together (Morgan, 1962 [1851]: 321–322).

Marriages were monogamous with one person married to only one other person at the same time. Indeed, Morgan (1962 [1851]: 824–825) indicates that polygamy was forbidden among the Iroquois or, in other words, a man could not have more than one wife at the same time. However, separation or divorce was permitted to all. The mothers of both parties tried to effect a reconciliation; but, if this did not work, a separation followed although this was infrequent due to pressure from public censure and the discredit it brought to the parties involved. Both the husband and wife maintained rights to their own property during marriage and in separation each took their holdings with them. In these instances, since the fathers were not part of the tribe of the children, no right of the father to the custody of children or responsibility for their upkeep was recognized. The relationship of the father to the children then became estranged as well as separated, as the father is indicated to no longer have had much contact with them. The care of infancy and childhood fell to the watchful affection of the mother alone (Morgan, 1962 [1851]): 325).

Likewise, the marriage residence pattern was matrilocal whereby the husband moved into his wife's residence. After the marriage contract was completed, he would unceremoniously move into his bride's mother's long house and she would offer him a customary welcoming bowl of hominy which marked his entry also into marriage and residence in her house. However, the new husband remained an important part of his own natal family and he would often visit his mother's and sisters' longhouse as overseer of their affairs and as guardian (Stockard, 2002: 65–68, 73–74).

Households could be of single bark houses suitable for one family of approximately eight and their provisions, when the village was scattered. When the village was compact, the houses were very long and subdivided to accommodate a number of families. The longhouse is recorded to be generally from fifty to a hundred and thirty feet in length, by about sixteen feet in width with partitions in intervals of about ten to twelve feet (Figure 5.3). Each compartment was like a separate house having a fire in the middle and it accommodated two families, one on each side of the fire. Therefore, a house that was one hundred and twenty feet long would contain ten fires and twenty families.

Morgan notes (1962 [1851]: 315–318) that one village called "Tiotohatton" had about 120 houses and that the largest of the Iroquois villages probably contained 3,000 inhabitants. The simple structure was called *Gä-no'-sote* or bark-house and consisted of five upright poles on the sides and four at the ends with cross-poles secured horizontally to which rafters, also poles, were attached. After the frame was ready, it was sided up and shingled with red elm or ask bark, the rough side out. In the roof was an opening for smoke from a fire in the center of the structure without a chimney; and, whatever the size of the structure, only two doors were found at either ends. Over one of these doors was cut the tribal symbol (totem) of the head of the family.

The subsistence strategy or adaptation of the Iroquois is identified as being horticultural and can be characterized as simple farming without the use of a plow, extensive irrigation systems, or intensive use of fertilizers (Stockard, 2002: 61). No individual could obtain absolute title to the land (no private property) as that was vested according to Iroquois laws in all people. However, a man could cultivate unoccupied lands and as long as he continued to use them, his right to their produce was protected. He could also sell his produce or bequeath them to his wife or children. If the wife inherited, either before or after marriage, orchards or plant lots or land for cultivation, she could also dispose of these as she pleased and at the time of her death, they were inherited with her other possessions by her children. However, when a father died by law, property could not pass out of the tribe and could not go to his children. Now if he gave planting lots or other property to his children or wife while alive in the presence of a witness, they could keep them. But if he made no plans for the dispossession of his property upon death, the property went to near relatives of his own tribe but who usually assigned the house to the family and other such articles as deemed advisable and distributed the rest among themselves as remembrances of the deceased (Morgan, 1962 [1851]: 326–327).

Women often did most of the horticultural work and provided the principal part of the family's subsistence. Women were also responsible for the preparation of the main meal. Male members of the long house, including unmarried lineage sons and the spouses of lineage daughters, did make economic contributions including from hunting, fishing, or trading expeditions (Stockard, 2002: 67). There was a lot of variety in their food choices and the principle articles of food were cracked corn, skinned corn hominy, two or three varieties of corn bread, venison and other game, soups, succotash, charred and dried green corn prepared in various ways, wild fruit, ground nuts (*Apios tuberosa*), beans, and squashes. They also had various types of teas, one being made from the tips of hemlock boughs boiled in water and seasoned with maple sugar. Maple tea was also made from boiling the sap and seasoning it with sassafras root. Other spicy teas were made as well (Morgan, 1962 [1851]: 329–330).

With this brief review of the kinship system, descent and marriage patterns, and other aspects of the lifeways of the historic League of the Iroquois, it is hoped that an image of real living peoples has been created which can help us to see how these concepts, as defined in Anthropology, might actually play out. From here we will define these larger sociopolitical intra- and intercommunity structures that we have begun to see in this review of the kinship patterns of the League of the Iroquois. Now we go on to look at territorial units larger than those of the immediate family and definitions of the concepts of lineages, clans, tribes, chiefdoms, and states will be covered in the following Part II of the book, as will the sociopolitical entities termed "imagined communities" in the anthropological literature.

PART II

Which Flag Should I Fly on the Fourth of July?

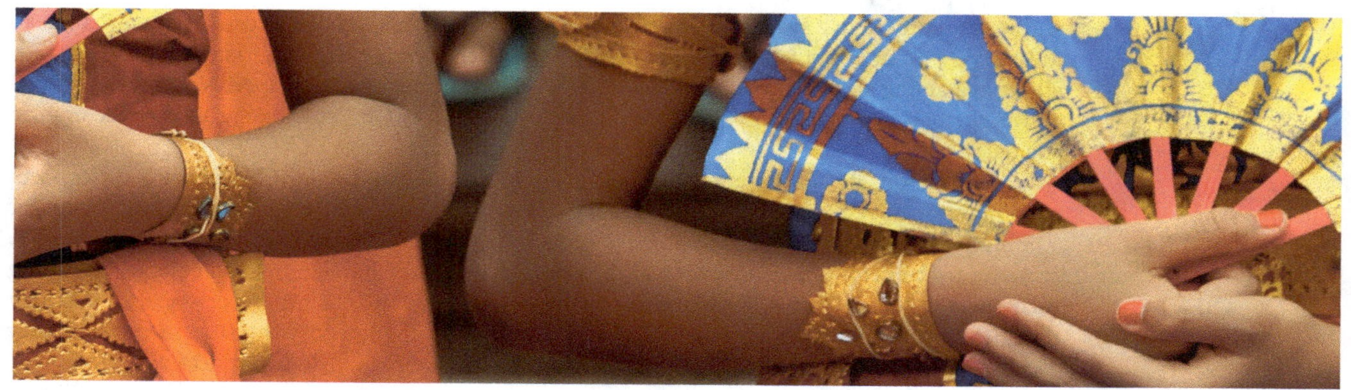

Chapter 6

The Individual, Social Identification, and Territoriality

Territoriality. Thank you to Drs. Bert Holldobler and Edward O. Wilson for writing about the concept of territoriality in ants back in 1990 (Holldobler and Wilson, 1990) when I was just starting to think about the movements of people and different political units over the landscape. Thank you also to Santiago Madriñán for helping us when Augusto Oyuela-Caycedo and I first met him in northern Colombia when we were starting our Ph.D. dissertations on the excavations of an archaeological site called San Jacinto 1, which ended up having the earliest fiber-tempered ceramics yet discovered in the Americas (Bonzani, 1995; Oyuela-Caycedo and Bonzani, 2005, 2014; Oyuela-Caycedo, 1987, 1993, 1995, 1996, 1998, 2001)! We met Santiago as he was just entering graduate school in a botany-related field at Harvard University to study with Dr. Wilson and he said when he sent him a letter introducing himself and his desire to go to Harvard, he included little specimens of different types of ants found in Colombia and, lo and behold, he was accepted! And he graduated! I also have to thank my many Professors at the University of Pittsburgh whom I took classes from in archaeology, cultural anthropology, and physical anthropology which helped me to write my first published book chapter on territorial manifestations in settlement patterns from tribal, chiefdom, and state-level societies as found on the island of Sardinia (Bonzani, 1992; Tykot and Andrews, 1992 in a volume dedicated to my first professor of archaeology at Tufts University, Dr. Miriam Balmuth). Territoriality seems to be a concept that can help us understand the movements of peoples on a landscape and their reactions to other groups also living and moving over landscapes in space and time.

First let's start with the individual and the premise that the individual is the unit upon which natural selection operates. One can start with this premise since it is individuals who reproduce and pass on genetic information in the form of genes and DNA. Natural selection, very basically, can be understood as forces that act upon the adaptation of individuals and species through time to their natural, cultural, social environments. A brief definition of natural selection is sometimes given as differential reproductive success of the individual and species in a given environment or landscape. The key term in this definition is the adjective differential. Not all individuals will have as many offspring as other individuals. Those individuals that have more offspring which are able to grow and reach reproductive age and then reproduce will pass on their genetic information more than an individual who does not have children or who has less children or who has many children but they all die at a young age. Generally, this is also applicable to a species in that species and their survival and perpetuation are affected by varying factors as they live in a landscape and these factors can change with time.

Many factors affect differential reproductive success. One of the most discussed is the concept of a limitation of resources; or stated a different way, populations will continue to expand except for a limitation of resources. The environment or landscape upon which an individual moves in space and over time affects that individual and the groups within which the individual belongs, including their species, access to resources. In this scenario individuals and the groups or societies to which they belong act in somewhat predictable ways in regards to the territory they live in and how they gain and defend resources of the territory. These actions which can include physical, social/political, economic, and religious manifestations can be understood by using the concepts of territoriality.

Territory can be defined as the domain or extent of land under the control of a group. Here, one sees that the individual may be the unit upon which natural selection works but individual humans are always parts of larger social groups. Again, these groups start with the nuclear family and then grow or expand from that. These groups can also be political units that control a territory and it often depends on the population size and subsistence strategies of the group that can help determine its political definition (Table 6.1) (see Bonzani, 2016; Table 24.1). If the population size is very small, the group could be a band; as population size and other economic activities that change the landscape increase, one may be looking at a tribe and chiefdom or in cases of very large populations with intensive manipulations of the landscape for food, one could be looking at a state. All of these units control a territory to varying degrees and some can be found even within the territorial boundaries of larger political units (i.e., a band might also be in the territory of a state like the Nukak-Makú bands found in the state of Colombia, South America).

Territoriality then is the collection of behaviors that the group exhibits in relation to the territory that the individual and group occupies. Important to this concept of territoriality is that it has both a spatial component and a temporal component so that sometimes the term is referred to as spatial-temporal territoriality. One may look at a snapshot of how a group uses a territory at a particular time (synchronic view), but as soon as time goes on the use of the territory can change (diachronic view). The spatial component of territoriality involves three basic concepts including the base, the range, and the boundaries. A fourth or fifth dimension can also occur which are more cosmological or ideological in nature and include physical locations known by the group but never or very rarely visited (occupied by nongroup members) and supraideological components which can include a spirit or supernatural realm which may or may not be visited by members of the group and from which entities or an entity may or may not have contact with the group or certain of its members. This would be where the religious beliefs of the group can come into play (Politis, 1996).

The base is the home or the area within which the individual and group most often spends its time. This can include the actual household or domicile and may or may not include how the group obtains food and/or money to maintain itself. It is the central location of where the group moves in its territory. The next level is the range and that is the area within which the individual and group travels. The travel can be to fields or to get water or wood or to go to work or school. It can be on a daily basis or as one gets further and further away from the base, the range traveled generally becomes less common until finally, one reaches the boundary or borders of the territory of the group. The boundaries are the borders of the territory through which the group and individual rarely travels. These are interesting areas and numerous anthropological studies have looked at these boundaries to see how different human groups interact and what happens at the intersection of the boundaries of two different groups (Barth, 1969; Cashdan, 1983, 1984, 1990a, 1990b, 1992; Wiessner, 1982 to list some of the earlier studies on this topic).

These boundaries can have different levels of what can be termed fluidity or permeability (Table 6.2). Depending on the sociopolitical structure of the groups under study, these boundaries can be very fluid and individuals and group members can move across them with relative frequency and ease. They are fluid and not well defined as is seen in band societies. As the political structure of the group becomes more complex and hierarchical, these boundaries can become

Table 6.1 General Components Involved in the Development of Complex Societies

	Type of Society	Hunter-Gatherer/Foraging	Horticulture/Pastoral	Agrarian	Industrial
	Population	- Small - ca. 50–100 people	- Medium - ca. 5,000–10,000 people or more	- Large - Over 10,000 to hundreds of thousands of people	- Large - Hundreds of thousands of people or more
	Culture	- Group identity markers	- Group identity and territorial markers - Ideologies of cults to the ancestors	- Group identity and territorial markers - Status differentiation - Ideological group markers	- Nationalism - Ethnic groups
	Material Products	-Rudimentary -Stone/Plant tools	-Rudimentary -Stone/Plant tools	- Plow - Milling devices - Metallurgy	- Industrial machines - Nonrenewable energy sources
Socioeconomic	**Energy Source**	- Human	- Human -Animal	- Human - Animal - Minimal machines (water/wind)	- Machines - Nonrenewable energy sources - Human/animal
	Control of Production	-Nuclear family (household)	-Nuclear family (household) - Kinship Linkages	-Nuclear family (household) - Kinship Linkages - Owner of land (Hereditary)	- Owners of machines/factories
	Location of Production	- Home territory	- Household - Village Territory	- Household - Community Territory (Cottage Industries)	- Factories outside of home and community
	Exchange Mechanism	- Generalized	- Generalized - Balanced (barter)	- Generalized - Balanced (barter) between communities - Development of negative exchange and a merchant class	- Negative (profit motive) - Merchant class controls transportation
	Payment for Labor	- "The gift"	- "The gift" - Higher status - Other products	- "The gift" - Higher status - Other products	- Money
	Status	- Egalitarian - Achieved status	- Ranked based on prestige - Achieved status - Start of ascribed status	- Stratified based on wealth, power, and prestige/status - Ascribed/Achieved - Classes/Castes	- Stratified based on wealth, power, and prestige/status -Often focused on wealth accumulation

Table 6.1 General Components Involved in the Development of Complex Societies (*continued*)

Type of Society	Hunter-Gatherer/Foraging	Horticulture/Pastoral	Agrarian	Industrial
Social-Political Institutions	- Kinship - Band - Extended Family - Social mechanisms of behavior control	- Kinship - Tribe - Lineages and clans - Social/ideological mechanisms of behavior control, arbitration	- Chiefdoms and States - Theocracies/ Nobility (ruler believed to be a God) - Rule-centered legal codes	- Shift toward democracies + individual human rights
Political Institutions	- Band - Egalitarian	-Tribal -Ranking - Development of chiefdoms	- Chiefdoms - Development of states - Stratification	- States - Stratification
Religious Ideologies	- Animism	- Animism - Magic - Totemism (ancestor worship)	- Totemism (ancestor worship) - Development of monotheism/polytheism	- Monotheism - Polytheism

Table 6.2 Expected Settlement Pattern and Range/Boundary Characteristic for Entities of Varying Sociopolitical Complexity

Sociopolitical Complexity	Settlement Pattern	Range/Boundary Characteristics
Egalitarian	Dispersed	Fluid
Chiefdom (prestate ranked)	Nucleated	Discrete (buffer zones present)
State (within borders)	Dispersed but compartmentalized	Discrete (single large center)

Source: From *Bare Backbones: A Brief Introduction to Anthropology* by Renée M. Bonzani. Copyright © 2015 by Cognella Academic Publishing. Reprinted by permission.

more rigid and fixed in space as seen in chiefdoms and states and movement across these boundaries must often be negotiated in some form with the group into which one is attempting to move (Bonzani, 1992). This negotiation can be asking permission from a contingent of people who have come to meet you at the boundary or in complex states it can be asking permission to enter a different country or state by obtaining a Visa for that country.

One can see that spatial boundaries are therefore affected by the types of societies into which one is born. All of these social institutions create forms of identity which are also associated to the subsistence base of the society so that one can define a sociopolitical institution and next to it list a general population size and general types of subsistence that are practiced by the people in that level of sociopolitical development. Three basic levels can be discussed with the first one already touched upon in previous chapters. These include:

1. The family level.
2. The community level.
3. The intercommunity level including the political units referred to for reasons of simplified categorization as bands, tribes, chiefdoms, and states.

Each of these has its own territorial size, identity, subsistence strategies, economic, political, and religious permutations (Table 6.1) (see Bonzani, 2016; Table 6.1). As indicated, the first family level has already been discussed in earlier chapters. In the next chapter a brief review of the community level including different kinship units and intercommunity level will be reviewed, so that one understands these basic concepts as used in Anthropology and in helping to explain cultural diversity.

The temporal component of territoriality is affected by both internal and external factors to individuals and the group or society to which they belong. These factors can be environmental and they can be sociocultural. In terms of some environmental factors, these can include seasonality or yearly changes in the climate based on things like fluctuations in temperature and precipitation or they can be longer-term changes to the environment due to climatic reasons or humans' past effects on a particular landscape.

Seasonality includes yearly somewhat predictable changes to the climate like rainy and dry seasons or winter and summer seasons. Different societies will adjust on the landscape to these changes, as for instance, bands will move to different parts of their territorial range depending on whether it is the rainy or dry season. Pastoralist and transhumant groups who move animals to different food resources (or follow the animals as they move) also travel around the landscape and the territories to which they have access depending on the season of the year. These are called nomadic, mobile, and/or semisedentary societies. More sedentary societies where people live basically in the same location all year long for numerous years also display seasonal mobility patterns, as for instance, during religious holidays and pilgrimages when large groups of people may travel to a religious shrine or sacred site. These religious times of the year often coincide with particular seasons as is the well-known example of Easter in Christianity which always occurs in spring and is associated to new growth, renewal, rebirth, and generally corresponds to the spring or vernal equinox of March 21 when in the northern hemisphere the sun lines up over the Equator and the orientation of earth's tilt in relation

Figure 6.1 Christmas in Cuzco, Peru December 25.
©Peek Creative Collective/Shutterstock.com

to the sun begins to point and be closer to the sun. Christmas in Christianity as identified in many denominations as occurring on December 25 indicates the birth of Christ and is also linked to the changing seasons and many important religious ceremonies and pilgrimages to holy sites. Close to this date is December 21 which is the winter solstice in the northern hemisphere that indicates (finally) based on the orientation of the earth's tilt and position around the sun, the northern hemisphere will be closer to the sun and summer is coming! (Figure 6.1)

Longer-term climatic changes are still very hard for humans to predict even with modern technologies and the ability to define climatic change in the past based on historical records or scientific research on such things as ice cores that can be used to determine the amounts of rainfall during a time period in relation to differences in oxygen isotopes. Still it is hard to know exactly what the climate will be like in a given area 20 years, 50 years, 100 years, 200 years from now.

Because of this and the inability of scientists and political-religious leaders in the past to predict and control or change weather patterns, a number of territorial changes can take place. One example could include state-level complex societies of the past when unusual drought conditions occurred for long periods of time. As indicated through research at Tiwanaku in the Bolivian altiplano near the capital of La Paz, these ancient ruins were once the central city and core of a probable state that existed from ca. C.E. 500 to ca. C.E. 1100 (Figure 6.2). After that time the city is eventually abandoned, the territorial aspects of its control over a wide area from preset day Peru, Bolivia, and Chile, decline and this complex society collapses. The probable reasons for this are now believed to be due to long-term climate change which resulted in long periods of drought (Janusek, 2002; Kolata, 2002, 1993; Kolata and Ortloff, 1996). The lack of rain decreased agricultural production utilized to support the large city population and hierarchy. The political-religious leaders had no control over this which eventually led to the collapse of this social-political- religious manifestation at that time period in that area of the world. Here, we see a spatial territory of a society expand and then collapse into smaller spatial units associated to possible homestead configurations and later chiefdoms or small kingdom territories in the same general area.

One example of how social factors might influence group territoriality takes us back to marriage. Since future generations are the ones who will be in the society's or group's territory in the future and will have use and control over it, sometimes there will be a lot of social pressure related to who one can and cannot marry. Reproduction is not only sexual; it includes sociocultural reproduction and the people of a society or group have culture, values, norms, and rules, that one could imagine they want to continue on into time. This sociocultural reproduction is done through example and education to offspring of these cultural values, beliefs, norms, and rules. One certainly can see why a person might not be happy to hear that their son or daughter is going to marry someone from a different background, culture, class, or religion. One often sees many ways in which the "status quo" is

Figure 6.2 Ruins of the Kalasasaya of the Ancient City of Tiwanaku, Bolivia, with Modern Town and Catholic Church in Background.
Source: Renée M. Bonzani, July 2008.

maintained or attempted to be maintained in the different aspects of a society and marriage rules are one of those ways. As covered in earlier chapters, in many societies marriages are arranged and the associated rules can be endogamous (marriage within the particular group) or exogamous (marriage outside of the particular group). Also in many societies one's status, wealth, and power is ascribed and regulated by birth. A society clearly needs resources and a territory to live in and these things need to be maintained through time. Also within the society the access to resources is maintained by other internal territories that can be regulated through such rules as endogamy and exogamy when applied to marriage. This is just one example of how the "status quo" might be maintained in a territory and through time. From this one can see that this regulation of spatial and temporal affiliations of an individual usually occurs so that the group or society to which the individual belongs can maintain control over key resources such as land, labor, and other important aspects in terms of survival and/or economic gain.

Another point that becomes evident is that these spatial boundaries for an individual and society can change, then, over time. Individuals may choose to leave one's group's territory and become a member of another group. An example would be a person who wants to migrate to a different country and become a citizen of that country and a member of the individuals who associate and are associated to a particular territorial unit (such as a state). Sometimes people are forced to do this and they have no choice. Larger political units can be created as in the creation over time of the current boundaries of the United States or they can be broken down as was seen in the example of the ancient territorial influences of Tiwanaku. Many, many other examples of this process can be found by looking at history or prehistory in all areas of the world.

Finally, with the use of symbols one can communicate their identity to others. Symbols tell us who someone is and who I am. Symbols are utilized to mark individual and group identities. A symbol is defined as an object used to represent something abstract. Through the use of objects that convey certain meanings, individuals or groups can mark that they belong or do not belong to a certain group. They can also be marked by member of another group as not being of that other group. Identity is who or what a person is. This differentiation between us and them seems to be a fundamental tenet of relations between humans and between human groups and is tied to the concept of territoriality and the access and control of resources in a particular territory and over time.

Chapter 7

The Origins and Diversification of Sociopolitical Systems

Bands, Tribes and Chiefdoms, and States

Community Level of Societies: From Egalitarian to Stratified

How are families organized through kinship? Briefly, one can trace the lines of a family both lineally and laterally. In Anthropology the lineal lines include the lineage and the clan. These can be traced temporally both back and forward in time; or in other words, lineal relatives are those from ascending and descending generations from the father's or mother's side including offspring. There is also a spatial component in that generally lineages and members of a clan live close by in the same territory. Laterally, this includes relatives basically associated to you, who one can term ego, on both your mother's side of the family and your father's side of the family; or, in other words, lateral relatives are kin on the side of the brother and sister of the mother and father. The interactions within these units, that is, between ego and his/her parents or grandparents or cousins, and between these units, that is, lineage or clan relations, are what earlier we placed in the community level of societies. This community level of societies can basically be found in three aspects which occur in a continuum and follow along with the concept of complexity including increasing population, intensification of food-getting strategies, and increasing hierarchies and specialization. These three aspects found on this continuum are termed egalitarian societies, ranked societies, and stratified societies.

Egalitarian Societies

One can think of egalitarian societies as ones in which there is equal access to resources by all members of the society. Status, power, and wealth differences do not occur or are minimal. These types of societies are generally termed bands or hunter-gatherers or foraging societies since they acquire their food from just that, foraging and collecting wild plants or animals and hunting and fishing wild animals. There may be some use of managing techniques, like clearing unwanted vegetation along a trail so that useful plants can grow, like edible palms. Even a limited amount of horticulture can occur whereby the landscape is purposefully and noticeably altered to make small gardens for the use of semi- and fully domesticated plants, that is, gardens for manioc, maize, plantain, etc. The use of these gardens is generally minimal since people in bands are highly mobile and move frequently, perhaps even every day to where resources are available.

Bands are comprised on two units: the nuclear family and the band which is when more than one nuclear family comes together for various reasons such as for festivals or in locations where food might be abundant at certain times of the year. These groups are very aware of their environments and territories and have routes or trails that they use frequently. Band territories or ranges may overlap with those of other bands since the boundaries between groups can be fluid. However, it appears to be that the people in a band basically know when they are entering another group's territory. They are also very aware of the temporal component of their territories as changes in seasonality are directly related to their movements and cohesion and dispersion into nuclear family units (Cabrera et al., 1999; Politis, 1996).

Foraging bands have little ascribed status and power and little authority differentiation. This will be defined later but basically it means that no one is born into a position of status, privilege, or power. Achievements are key in these societies as to determining if someone has status or is greatly respected or if they have power and people will follow them and do what they ask. For instance, a good hunter will have prestige for this fact and people will follow him/her on a hunt because they know the person knows what they are talking about and has had good results in hunting (Lee, 1979).

Ranked Societies

Ranked societies are those societies that are comprised of kinship groups that vary in status, prestige, or social esteem. Prestige can be defined as esteem based on social relations, usually by people in neighboring communities and kinship structures such as lineages and clans. It is identified as not being a physical resource (Clark and Blake, 1994). One might also view these societies as traditional types of societies as the individual's access to resources is based on their kinship group. These societies that function in relation to the kinship group are what Durkheim (1947 [1893]) referred to as mechanical societies and egalitarian and stratified societies can also be organized in this way.

In ranked societies one can find the lineage and the clan. The lineage is defined as a consanguineal kin group practicing unilineal descent, both of patrilineal and matrilineal descent groups. The lineage includes persons who can trace their descent to a common ancestor. In other words, a lineage is all of the unilineal descendants of a known common ancestor or ancestors. Here it is important to stress the fact that this is a known common ancestor such as a grandfather, grandmother, or great-grandmother and great-grandfather. They are either still alive or someone actually remembers them when they were alive. This fact helps one to place lineages in time and space. Lineage members may all live in the same community or close by villages or towns. In time the living memory goes back one, two generations linking all descendants as belonging to the same lineage (see Cole 1975 for an example of Bedouin lineages in Saudi Arabia).

Tracing descent in ranked societies becomes more important, it seems, the more the different kinship units in the society are differentially ranked. In bands and hunter-gatherers, the living memory of ancestors sometimes only goes back one to two generations. The time depth of these units is much shorter. In some ranked societies time depth of ancestor relations can go back many, many generations and hundreds of years which can eventually lead to ascribed societies like chiefdoms, where to become a chief one must be born into the appropriate kin group whose ancestors play (they become spirit entities) and played a role in building and maintaining the status, power, and wealth of the group.

When peoples trace descent back many, many generations and hundreds of years, one is looking at what in Anthropology and in English is termed a clan. The society itself may have a term in its own native language which is identifying basically the clan or clans of that group. For instance, the term *ayllu* utilized by Quechua-speaking indigenous groups in the Andes Mountains is believed to have a similar concept as that of the clan (Janusek, 2002b; Murra, 1980, 1972). A clan is defined as a descent group whose members claim descent from a common apical ancestor but they cannot demonstrate it; it is sometimes referred to as stipulated descent. The ancestor lived so long ago that no one (still living) really knew the person. A clan, therefore, is a group of lineages, all of which trace descent back to a common ancestor (Oyuela-Caycedo, 2000).

Furthermore, one can think of a clan as a compromise kin group based on a rule of residence and a rule of descent. The adjective compromise is used here to indicate that this relationship can be fictive. An actual blood line to the clan is not necessary as one can be made a clan member even if you are not born into the clan. This membership may be based off of necessity and/or honor and sometimes can take on a patron/client type of relationship whereby the client asks for permission to be part of the clan from the elders or headman/chief/lord. The client will supply things like food, labor, and other goods to the headman/chief/lord and in exchange may acquire protection and other benefits in a particular territory.

Since these ancestors, then, become spirit entities themselves, they interact with other spirit entities in the cosmology of the society. These other spirit entities can be anthropomorphized or not. They are important because they control what can happen to an individual and the groups that they are part of, as for instance they give food, water, and things like rain. These gifts must be reciprocated by humans and their societies. Many of these groups then have shaman and other important individuals to the community who can act as intermediaries with the spirit entities.

Masked dances are associated rituals that can be found in these societies as the masked dancers represent the spirits that are important to the group. These spirit entities then can become associated to certain groups of people based on their clan membership and they interact with or become one with the ancestors of that group, which is a kinship group, the clan. Therefore, clans are often represented by animals or plants that are important to the society and the clan becomes associated with the powers of that animal or plant (Descola, 1996, 1994). When that happens, in Anthropology this is referred to as a totem (Figure 7.1). A totem is when the clan's apical ancestor is nonhuman. Just as animism is a religious practice associated to a belief in spirit entities; totemism is a religious practice defined as a cult to the ancestors who are not dead but are interacting with or are represented by the totem and who have an effect on their living descendants.

Besides the lineage and the clan, a society can also be separated into two divisions. Moieties are when a society is divided into two groups so that every one person is necessarily a member of one or the other moiety. Claude Leví-Strauss (1964) noted these structural sociopolitical arrangements in numerous indigenous groups that he encountered in his early days of fieldwork in South America. For the Tikuna indigenous group in the Amazon Basin living within and across the territorial boundaries of Colombia, Peru, and Brazil, each person is a member of a clan but they are also a member of a moiety so that certain clans are members of the moiety associated to the sky and other clans are associated to the moiety or division of the society linked to the earth (Nimuendajú, 1952; Oyuela-Caycedo and Vieco, 1999).

In some instances, moiety members may live in different parts of the same community. In the Andes leaders of both moieties are involved in decision-making practices (in the politics) of the society (Platt, 2006). In terms of marriage practices, one must usually marry someone from the other moiety in your community (exogamy). It is believed that this allows for access of different clans and family members to resources that they may not be able to have access to, otherwise. For instance, if a daughter has to marry outside of her moiety and move to a village/town in a different elevation zone, then her family will be able to have access to resources in that zone and she will be able to supply access to resources from her family's elevational ecozone. When she has her own children and they belong to one moiety and are required to marriage outside of the moiety (exogamy), then the daughter will have to marry into the different lower elevational moiety and the cycle repeats itself, almost like a ladder being built through time and involving kinship, marriage, clans, moieties, larger tribal or chiefdom societies, and the need for resource acquisition (Figure 7.2).

Forms of Rank

How are people ranked within a society? Ranking in a society can include ascribed and achieved positions and it can also depend on one's age. As indicated previously, ascribed positions are those that one is born into at birth. They are inherited through the line of one's kinship group. The inheritance can be unilineal (patrilineal or matrilineal) or it can be bilineal or ambilineal. Achieved positions or rank are those that are obtained through age, consensus, or merit. In fact, one of the ways that archaeologists try to determine if a society is a tribe or a chiefdom is to look for signs of ascribed status or position. Such signs in the archaeological record include finding burials of young children

Figure 7.1 Northwest Coast Indigenous Totem Poles Moved to Burke Museum, University of Washington, Seattle. July 2016.
Source: Renée M. Bonzani.

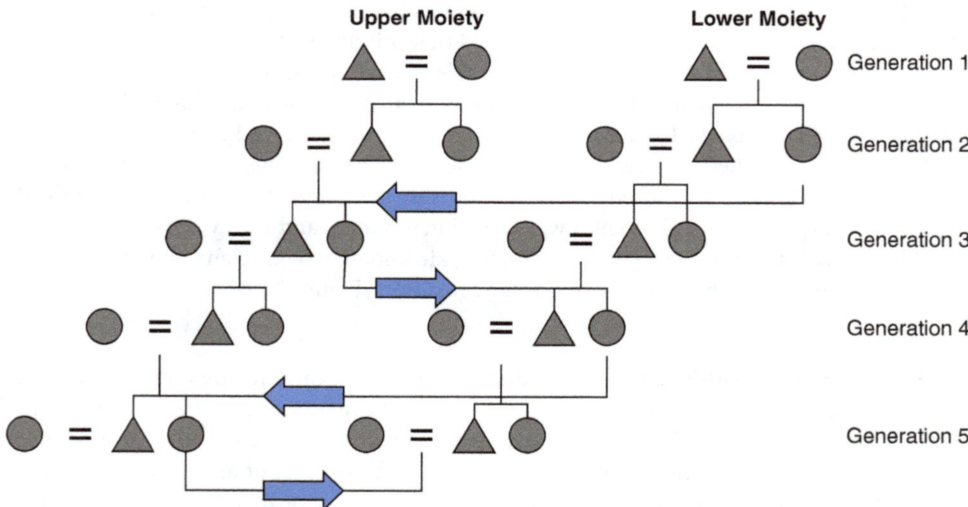

Figure 7.2 Hypothetical Kinship Diagram of Exogamous Marriage Patterns in Moieties.

or adolescents that have numerous amounts of burial goods that they could not have achieved or accumulated in their own short lifetimes. When the ability to hold a political standing or office is based on birth or birthright, then one is looking at a chiefdom (see below for definition).

Hunter-gatherer groups as mentioned demonstrate achieved status for individuals as generally do tribal societies. In some instances, one's position in the society may be based off of both ascribed and achieved statuses. One may not be born into a particular position of high rank but based on exceptional achievements or honor, one might be placed into that position by the community or by important members of the community (for one example from Micronesia in the south Pacific Ocean see Ward 2005).

Age is another way that a person can be ranked within a society. Anthropologists have identified age sets and age grades in many if not all societies. Age sets are groups of individuals that share the characteristics of being born in the same time span, for instance five years. Their position in a society and community is defined by their age set. These individuals usually participate in rituals and go through the different stages of life at the same time as members of the same age group. For instance for the indigenous pastoralist Nuer of eastern Africa, adolescent boys when they reach puberty and are ready to become adults will go through the rites of passage together that is called *gar*. In these rites of passage, a series of rituals are performed which include separating the young men and preparing them for the next stage of rituals, for instance cutting the hair and removing any jewelry from the body (preliminal or stage of separation). The young men then go through a transitory stage or liminal stage which involves scarring the young man's head, indicated to be done by a visiting shaman, to mark that he has become a man. After resting overnight or perhaps longer, the young men have entered the postliminal stage of incorporation and a feast is held to welcome them back into the community as new adult male members after which they can acquire a new name, and cattle, and take on a wife (Evans-Pritchard, 1940; for the stages of a ritual see Van Gennep, 2004 [1908]).

Age grades are the sequence of statuses of these age sets. Generally, these will run from juniors, seniors, to elders with juniors including adolescents and unmarried men and women. Seniors include married men and women, usually of a certain age and often with children or junior members still in the household. Elders are the oldest members of the community and may serve as advisors in regards to important decisions that are made that will affect the group or community as a whole. For instance, for the indigenous group of the Dani who live in the Grand Valley Dani of Irian Jaya, Indonesia (West New Guinea), in the past during the stylized ritual warfare or clan feuding, it was the young unmarried junior men who go to the fields first and are actively engaged in taunting the enemy. The senior men hang back, may arrive late to the field, and are often the one's giving directions during the fighting or feuding (Heider, 1970).

Feuding is defined as chronic hostilities between groups, neighbors, or kin and can continue from one generation to the next. When killing does occur, it is referred to as a blood feud and usually initiates and requires revenge for the death of a kinsman. The revenge may take the form of the murder of kin from the killing person's patrilineage so that the actual killer does not have to be the one killed; a brother, sister, and even child will avenge the death. In some instances, a negotiated settlement, such as cattle, other products, or cash can be given by the killer's extended family in replacement of further violence. These are sometimes called blood money or blood payments (Evans-Pritchard, 1940).

Stratified Societies

What is the difference between societies that are ranked or in which one's position is based on the rank of the kinship group (lineage, clan) and those societies which are even more complex and are identified as stratified? In these societies one has to look for the creation of separate strata. This is called stratification. All ancient and modern state-level societies, for instance, are stratified. It is part of the definition of a complex society: A complex society has a hierarchy (in some cases stratification), specialization, and functional differentiation of the different aspects of the society. In archaeology when one looks at prehistoric and historic states, they always have a hierarchy and stratification. Their populations level are very large, perhaps today in the millions to billions of people and there must be intensive (large amounts of energy input, be it through human and/or animal labor or machines that need alternative forms of energy to run) ways to obtain food. The emergence of stratification indicates the transition from chiefdom to state (Kottak, 2013: 390–391).

A stratum is one of two or more groups that are contrasted in terms of status and access to resources. Each stratum has people of all ages and both sexes or of all gender or nongender affiliations. Max Weber (1992/1968) identified three dimensions to social stratification:

1. Prestige or the basis of social status refers to esteem, respect and approval for acts, deeds, or other qualities thought of as exemplary.
2. Power or the ability to exercise one's will over others or to get others to do things.
3. Economic status or wealth including a person's material assets.

From archaeology, as indicated above it appears to be that differences between individuals in a society actually begin in relation to the concept of status. Individuals and kinship groups can gain or achieve a higher ranking in a society by doing something that the community considers important and this adds status or prestige to them. This is hard to identify in the archaeological record since status does not equate with material possessions. People of high status may have very little material possessions. Indeed, in many chiefdom societies like the Northwest Coast indigenous groups of the United States and Canada, the way to maintain the position of chief was to redistribute and even give away gifts during festivals. Accumulation of material wealth was frowned upon and could lead to a person losing their status as a chief (Boas, 1940).

The chief was not just a figurehead and although he or she would receive tribute and gifts from members of their community or chiefdom, they had to reciprocate by providing numerous things such as food, cloth, and other material possessions; but, perhaps most importantly, they had to conduct rituals and be in contact with the supernatural entities to secure the social and biological reproduction of the group. They were also in charge of both the physical and spiritual protection of the group. If this reproduction or continuation of the group was perceived to be in jeopardy, the chief could lose his or her political position. In some instances another form of a chief, one more secular and militaristic, might arise and gain power (Santos-Granero, 1986).

Whether power differences or wealth differences arise next seems to be hard to say. One needs to have power to get people to do things which can lead to wealth accumulation. However, wealth can also equate with power in that to get something done, one can also use wealth payments to accomplish this and status may also not have anything to do with whether or not someone will work or follow a person. At least in the modern industrial societies, people will do almost anything for money and it makes no difference what the status of the person is who is offering the money. As long as they have accumulated enough wealth, power may follow.

There are in general two types of stratified societies: castes and classes. Castes are defined in Anthropology as societies to which membership and types of labor are ascribed at birth and in which social mobility between groups or sets is not allowed. Examples of societies identified as having castes occur in India and illustrate a strong separation between the different strata of a society even to the point that the religion seems to reinforce the notion of moving from one caste to another only through the process of reincarnation and perhaps karma (Dumont, 1970).

A class is defined not by kinship primarily but by the degree of access to valued resources in a society, namely, wealth, power, and prestige. Class is usually defined in economic terms. Marx (1867; Marx and Engels, 1848) recognized two divisions in class societies: the bourgeoisie, which owns the means of production (tools, knowledge, and raw materials), and the proletariat, or working class, which owns their labor power.

For a basic understanding of this, one needs to review economic interactions from the point of view of Production Theory, sometimes also referred to as the Marxist approach, as briefly mentioned in earlier chapters. In this theory, there are three interrelated components:

1. Labor which is the activity linking human social groups to the material world of production.
2. Means of production which are the tools or means to produce materials, or goods and also including perhaps the most important means of production, land.
3. Modes of production which is a characterization of the relationship between labor, the means of production, and who controls the means of production.

Depending on how these three things are related, different economic and political structures occur and examples include feudal, capitalist, primitive communist, socialist mode of production. The class within which one finds him or herself will be based on whether they or their kinship group or in the case of communism, the nonrelated community members, own or control the means of production (the bourgeoisie) or whether they are the laborers and own their own labor (the proletariat). The tensions and relations between these two groups can result in shifts in the sociopolitical structure of the society as, for instance, when feudalism in Europe reached such a state of inequality between the bourgeoisie and the proletariat that revolutions occurred to overthrow the monarchies of many of those countries (i.e., the French and Russian Revolutions). Another example of class societies are modern industrial societies like the United States. In these types of societies due to the competitive nature of capitalism and a good education system, these classes are not fixed in stone and generally one can move up or down in class depending on achievements, unlike in caste societies that are based on ascribed status and position of the individual in the society.

Intercommunity Level: Variation in Political Organization

In this section, the definitions of bands, tribes, chiefdoms, and states as political units that occupy a territory in space and time are defined. In these structures one can find positions of power which require leadership. Leadership is characterized by the capacity to mobilize other individuals into action. It is an achieved form of power. Great Men or Big Men are characterized as individuals that because of their achievements in warfare or hunting maintain the political office of a group and examples of this can be found in the Baruya and the Etoro of Papua New Guinea. Chiefs as indicated are ascribed positions, by inheritance through the relationship and position to the dominant kin of a political unit.

Bands

Bands are the oldest form of political organization, characterized by being of small scale (up to 50 to 100 individuals), that depend on gathering and hunting. Power is achieved. For examples see the !Kung San (South Africa) (Lee, 1970), the Maku (Brazil, Colombia, and Venezuela) (Cabrera et al., 1999), and Mbuti (Zaire).

Tribes

Tribes are horticultural/pastoral groups where there is competition for power between kin groups, such as clans that may have feuding between their members. Traditionally, they are generally small in demographic scale, and power is limited to the settlement. Each settlement occupied by related persons could be considered an independent autonomous unit who makes their own political decisions. These autonomous kinship units may in times of threat or stress join together to form the larger political and territorial unit known as the tribe, as identified by Evans-Pritchard (1940) for the pastoralist groups of the Nuer in eastern Africa. For further example see the Yanomami (southern Venezuela and northern Brazil.) (Chagnon, 1983) and the indigenous groups of highland West New Guinea (Irian Jaya of Indonesia) (Heider, 1970).

Chiefdoms or Rank Societies

Chiefdoms are political structures based on ascribed positions based on lineage or rank of individuals controlling an area through alliances by marriage and warfare. The chiefs monopolize the use of force by maintaining a section of the society that specializes in warfare. They also are able to organize a system of tax collectors, as well, to collect tribute which may be in the form of edible and nonedible products and/or labor. Sometimes those individuals that are captured in war are incorporated as slaves.

It is difficult to find examples of chiefdoms existing in the modern world today, if any actually still do exist (Figure 7.3). This difficulty is because chiefdoms and the power of the chief is eliminated in state societies as power is centralized and cannot occur in numerous individuals in numerous territories at the same time. The chief and chiefdom are threats to the power of the state. In these cases, the chief may be killed or he or she may be adopted into the "family" of the ruling elite and become a

Figure 7.3 Chief Regulo Moquepera, his Two Sons and Some of his Wives. Portuguese Africa ca. 1900. Coll. Monas Hierogliphica, Milan.
Source: Monti, Nicolas, ed. *Africa Then. Photographs 1840-1918.* New York: Alfred A. Knopf, 1987.

representative to his/her people of the overarching controlling influence of the state. Arranged marriages and building political alliances through marriage can also be found as a way to incorporate a chiefdom into a larger political unit. For examples of chiefdoms in the archaeological record of South America, for instance, see Moore (2014).

States

The state is a political unit that controls a usually large territory. There are many aspects and characteristics of a state. Two of the most commonly cited are that the state is the agency or agencies within a society that have the monopoly over the legitimate use of violence. The state is also associated to a centralization of power. Other characteristics include communication and transportation networks, an intensive subsistence base, writing or other means of accounting systems, territorial control of land based on defined partitioning of lands and peoples, specialization of labor and stratification, as mentioned earlier, ranking or hierarchical ordering of classes and kinship networks, ideological belief often in a Creator God with lesser ranking Gods (ancient states), redistribution and trade, and monumental architecture (Bonzani, 2016: Table 14.1).

Chapter 8

Political and Social Identification

Indigenous Groups, Ethnicity, the State, and Nationalism

In this chapter we have to address the issues of ethnicity and nation-states, so we have to move beyond these older definitions of sociopolitical structures given in the previous chapter and redefine them based on the fact that we live in a very interconnected world sometimes referred to as globalization. To do this, one should still keep in mind the concepts of spatial-temporal territoriality because humans are still animals that display these traits but now these behaviors have to be incorporated into sociopolitical units that might encompass a billion people in one territorial entity!

To review, we started with the individual that moves in space and through time on a landscape. This human by necessity is linked to a family; one has to be born somehow and this will involve usually male and female parents, but in the modern world it can involve two male or two female parents or one parent that has a child or children. Beyond this, we outlined larger kinship units like the lineage and clan that also occupy a space on the landscape and generally trace time backward and forward through descent relations. We now have to move beyond these smaller kinship units to address the varieties of arrangements of groups of people that Anthropologists use to try to explain various types of behaviors and relations within and between groups.

Imagined Communities

The term "imagined communities" refers to groups of people who are organized into sociopolitical units whose constitution or makeup can change with external and internal forces and the perception of the individual. These sociopolitical configurations are not written in stone. They can change and people can move in and out of them based on their own decisions or the decisions of others. They are imagined; they are forms of organization which again appear and can disappear through time and whose boundaries and borders can change through time. They are involved in social reproduction and to be successful must guarantee the biological reproduction or the potential thereof, as well, of members of the specific group under question. Early works on these concepts can be found in Anderson (1983) and Barth (1969). For this chapter, the definitions and examples found in

Maybury-Lewis's very informative book "Indigenous Peoples, Ethnic Groups, and the State" (2002), that is now out of print (as I was told when trying to reorder this book for classes), are utilized in this chapter to try to explain sometimes very vague definitions about these concepts.

The term "culture" had been used more so in Anthropology to describe a group of people who had similar customs and since the end of the nineteenth century, the concept of culture seems to be related to knowledge and beliefs that are learned (Tylor, 1871). Later in the beginning of the twentieth century, the concept changed to that related to the habits or behaviors that are learned and reproduced by the group (Boas 1938 [1911]). In Anthropology today, the term culture has largely been replaced by the term ethnicity that is used to identify groups that have people who are linked together in certain ways, for instance usually but not always living in the same location or territory, and have similar languages, beliefs, and behaviors. In archaeology instead of saying culture, one might instead see the term horizon used which means a period of widely disseminated art and artifact styles believed to represent peoples with similar beliefs, either of the same political unit but possibly also belonging to different political units (Pool, 2007).

The terms used in many anthropological text today to describe these sociopolitical entities are: indigenous groups, ethnic groups, states, and nations. Each of these will be discussed below with one or two examples from peoples living around the world today.

Indigenous Groups

In Maybury-Lewis (2002: 6), indigenous peoples can be defined as those that claim their lands because they were there first or have occupied them since time immemorial. They were there first and therefore have "rights of prior occupancy to their lands." Again, there is a spatial aspect in terms of the extent of control of a territory by a particular group of people and there is a temporal aspect in that these are the first peoples to occupy the land. This distinction can be necessary when colonizers move into a new territory to claim lands and the original people may have no written land deeds or records of ownership. They can work with nongovernmental organizations (NGOs) by using this prior occupancy claim to maintain the rights to their lands. Maybury-Lewis gives the example of the Aborigines of Australia or the Maoris of New Zealand (Figure 8.1) as peoples or societies who are "indigenous" compared to recent settlers. In these cases, as with Native North Americans, the new settlers came much later.

However, in some parts of the world there have been numerous indigenous peoples that have moved back and forth over time in the same and different territories. These indigenous peoples have often been conquered or forced to move by other peoples of different ethnicity, cultures, and "racially"

Figure 8.1 The Maoris, Indigenous Peoples of New Zealand. Maori Women and Girls of a Kapa Haka (Traditional Dance) Group Doing a Poi Dance to Celebrate Waitangi Day. Tauranga, New Zealand. February 6, 2019.

as indicated by Maybury-Lewis (2002: 6). They are generally minorities within these larger political entities and struggle to maintain their cultures. Since they do not have their own states and are not main political decision-makers of the states they live in, they are generally referred to as tribal peoples also.

The phrase tribal peoples is imprecise and hard to define. In the previous chapter, a definition of the tribe was given. To add to this, tribal peoples today are generally defined as small-scale, preindustrial societies that live in comparative isolation and manage their affairs without any centralized authority, such as the state (Maybury-Lewis, 2002: 7). They generally live in marginal areas, like close to deserts or in high mountainous regions or tropical forests that are hard to get to with the most productive more accessible land being already taken over by a larger majority ethnic and/or indigenous group. Sometimes if they are really isolated, they may not even know that they are part of a state, as was the case with the Nukak-Makú, an indigenous group in the northwestern Amazon Basin, that until about twenty or thirty years ago had not had any contact with outsiders that is known of (Politis, 1996). The family structures such as lineages and clans then are the political decision-making entity and they may not follow the norms and rules of the wider state. Tribal groups in the mountainous regions of Afghanistan could be thought of as an example of this (Figures 8.2 and 8.3). To move through these territories one must go through different clan and tribal units, potentially asking for permission from the leaders of each to enter their territories even though the territories are also part of the state of Afghanistan with a centralized capital in Kabul.

Further these groups are preindustrial which means basically that they do all of their work by using human or animal labor. The use of technology and machines is not widespread yet, adding somewhat to this sense of isolation. Tribal peoples then can be isolated and they are generally minorities within the states that they live in. Often, they have no or very little government representation: they do not have elected representatives who sit in on the state's discussions on policy or laws. Because of these various factors, they are often subject to the processes called ethnocide and genocide.

Figure 8.2 Indigenous Peoples in the Mountains of Afghanistan and Pakistan. Pashtun Tribal Members in the 1930s in What Is Now Pakistan and Afghanistan.

Figure 8.3 Afghan Tribal Members, from Gardez, Paktia, participate in a Jirga. August 26, 2009 in Gardez, Southeast Afghanistan to Discuss Pressing Issues.

Ethnocide is defined as the destruction of people's or societies' way of life (Maybury-Lewis, 2002: 7). Their way of life or culture (the totality of the behaviors, beliefs, norms, institutions that people acquire as members of a particular society) may not be condemned but their incorporation into the mainstream culture is seen as a way of civilizing the group since they are often viewed as backward, particularly if they do not use or have access to modern technology and machines. Their ways of like are in essence destroyed or changed to mimic that of the dominant culture or ethnic group.

The process of *indigenismo* initiated after the Mexican Revolution (1910–1920) is given as an example where lands were made accessible once again to communities and economic assistance and education were made available by the government to help these groups get rid of their backward ways and "Indianness," and join the national mainstream. In a world population of over 7 billion, Maybury-Lewis (2002: Table 1.1) estimates that 257,572,600 people belong to indigenous groups (as of 2002).

Taken to another level, all together, is genocide. Genocide is defined as the physical extermination of a defined category of people (Maybury-Lewis, 2002: 7). Genocide is universally condemned but as Maybury-Lewis (2002: 7) indicates it continues to happen today and is extremely difficult to prevent and to punish. One of the issues is that it is difficult to know who the defined category of people will be and it can be different in different circumstances based on current and historical factors for a particular region. This definition can be based on race or religion or even members of different classes or strata in a state. Again, in all instances we see the concept of "us" versus" them" become strongly forced, ingrained, brainwashed, or accepted into and by peoples who perceive themselves as being different. The promotion of these views seems to be based on the need for one group to eliminate the other group who is often perceived or referred to as nonhuman. One is not eliminating a human, one like ourselves, but these are animals, infidels, nonhuman savages who are a blight on the earth. How else could you get someone to shoot down or hatchet to death men without weapons and women and children?

The term "genocide" was first used in 1944 by Raphael Lemkin in a book called the "Axis Rule in Occupied Europe" to describe the horrors of the Holocaust which was the active incarceration and killing of peoples identified as different by Hitler and the Nazi Germans. Many people were gassed to death or starved to death in the concentration camps in Germany in World War II (Figure 8.4). These peoples included Jews from Germany and other parts of Europe and other ethnic groups like the Romani, colloquially known as Gypsies or Roma (an Indo-Aryan ethnic group). However, they were not considered to be part of the "Aryan race"; they were utilizing resources that should go to the German people. Propaganda promoted them as in essence nonhuman. In the bad economic times of the early 1900s in Europe, elimination of these groups was promoted as a way to solve the problem.

Figure 8.4 Inside of Building in Former Nazi Concentration Camp, located in Auschwitz I, Poland. ©photoshooter2015/Shutterstock.com

Museums made to commemorate those who died in the Holocaust can be found in a number of cities in the United States including in Washington, DC and also in Germany, itself. However, the act of genocide has continued to occur around the world.

To understand the Holocaust, one might want to watch the documentary called "Memory of the Camps." The producers warn that it is very graphic and disturbing and one should prepare themselves for this before viewing. The documentary is described as follows: "A documentary on the liberation of the German concentration camps was assembled in London in 1945 from footage shot by the service and newsreel cameramen accompanying the British, American, and Russian armies. The documentary was left unfinished, with missing sound tracks and a missing sixth reel. The directors, including Alfred Hitchcock, developed a script to go with the pictures, and in May 1985, FRONTLINE first presented this documentary" (https://www.pbs.org/wgbh/pages/frontline/teach/camps/). It is indicated to be unedited and as close as possible to what the producers intended sixty years ago.

Maybury-Lewis (2002: Chapter 3) also gives the examples of the genocide in Rwanda in 1994 which involved the ethnic groups of the Tutsis and Hutus (de Waal, 1994; Lemarchand, 1994) and the breaking apart of the former United Nations recognized state of Yugoslavia (Denitch, 1994; Djilas, 1991; Glenny, 1992; Heyden, 1995). Remember this is just a brief review of these internationally recognized cases of genocide. To see a documentary on the genocide in Rwanda see Frontline's "The Triumph of Evil." Here, it is worth reiterating the introduction to the film as listed by Frontline (https://www.pbs.org/wgbh/pages/frontline/shows/rwanda/reports/dsetexhe.html):

"Genocide is distinguishable from all other crimes by the motivation behind it. Towards the end of the Second World War, when the full horror of the extermination and concentration camps became public knowledge, Winston Churchill stated that the world was being brought face to face with 'a crime that has no name.' History was of little use in finding a recognized word to fit the nature of the crime that Nazi Germany, a modern, industrialized state, had engaged in. There simply were no precedents in regard to either the nature or the degree of the crime. Raphael Lemkin, the Polish-born adviser to the U.S. War Ministry, saw that the world was being confronted with a totally unprecedented phenomena and that 'new conceptions require new terminology.' In his book, Axis Rule in Occupied Europe, published in 1944, he coined the word 'genocide', constructed, in contradiction to the accepted rules of etymology, from the Greek 'genos' (race or tribe) and the Latin suffix 'cide' (to kill). According to Lemkin, genocide signifies 'the destruction of a nation or of an ethnic group' and implies the existence of a coordinated plan, aimed at total extermination, to be put into effect against individuals chosen as victims purely, simply and exclusively because they are members of the target group."

In central Africa this region known as Ruanda-Urundi had been ruled by Belgium from 1916 to 1962. These peoples in this area are known as Tutsi, Hutu, and Twa but they speak the same language, share the same religion and culture, and are indicated to have generally the same physical characteristics. However, to exaggerate economic class differences, such differences were supposedly related to separate racial backgrounds. The Tutsi was a term applied to wealthy family lineages that controlled wealth (mainly cattle) and power. Hutu lineages supposedly did not control wealth but were the peasants, although movements into either of these groups were possible based on wealth accumulation or the loss of wealth.

The Tutsi aristocracy was supported by the Colonial powers. Conflicts between these groups escalated until 1994 when President Habyarimana's plane was shot down and along with the President of Burundi, he was killed. The Presidential Guard set up a roadblock and began to kill anyone that was considered Tutsi including the Prime Minister of Rwanda and the Hutu ministers who tried to stop this. In the next few months Hutu extremists killed hundreds of thousands of Tutsi men, women, and children until the Rwandese Popular Front (FPR, initials of name in French) (Maybury-Lewis 2002: 84), made up of exiled Tutsi's in Uganda, defeated the Rwandan Hutu army. Estimates of the death toll reached half a million yet the outside world did not step in rapidly and pulled out United Nations' peacekeepers since initially this was seen as a civil war or "tribal conflict."

In the case of the former state of Yugoslavia, a different term came into use to describe the rampant killing of people that occurred after this state collapsed after the 1980s. This is a complicated area to track the movements of tribal peoples who spoke Slavic languages in the region in the sixth and seventh centuries. This area was a frontier zone between contending empires, religions, and civilizations. In the early 1900s, peoples identified as Slovenes, Croats, and Bosnians were ruled by the Austro-Hungarian Empire and Serbs and Macedonians were ruled by the Ottoman Empire centered in Turkey. They had intermingled and intermarried apparently for long periods of time. In 1929, however the kingdoms of the Serbs, Croats, and Slovenes were renamed Yugoslavia which brought together the people of the southern Balkans into a single state for the first time. In 1941, Yugoslavia was invaded by the Axis powers that dismantled the state and claimed parts of its territory. This started a process of genocide where, for instance, the Ustasa government of Croatia intended to create a Croatia inhabited only by Croatians. They planned following Nazi Germany to eliminate all Jews and Gypsies. The Serbs had a different fate. One-third were killed; one-third driven from their lands; and one-third would be converted to Catholicism, or to "de-Serbianize" them (Maybury-Lewis, 2002: 92).

Then, Yugoslavia was reconstituted as a state under the communist rule of President Tito, having six republics: Slovenia, Croatia, Serbia, Bosnia-Herzegovina (Bosnia), Montenegro, and Macedonia. In the 1980s a world economic downturn occurred. Tito himself died and nationalist leaders arose like Slobodan Milosevic who promoted that Serbia should be its own state for its own Serbian people. Once again, the other non-Serbians were viewed with hostility.

The Yugoslavian federation could not be saved and broke apart into a series of internal conflicts that have also taken on the name of "ethnic-cleansing." Ethnic cleansing is a practice of massacring people of a different ethnic group in order to clear their lands and take over their territory for settlement by the attackers (Maybury-Lewis, 2002: 97). In these cases, the people of an ethnic group are identified as different and their territory is usually identified as having first belonged to the original inhabitants which are the attacking group. The people of the ethnic groups are killed to "cleanse" (to "purify") the territory of them and to open the lands for new settlement by the other nationalist "pure" ethnic group. The North Atlantic Treaty Organization (NATO) and Russia finally stepped in to help to stop the fighting in Serbia, Croatia, Kosovo, and the massacre of Albanian and other ethnic groups in the Balkans region of Europe. Milosevic was finally voted out of power and the current configurations of states in this area was instituted.

Ethnicity and Ethnic Groups

Ethnicity is another concept that can be particularly hard to define as it is an imagined community. Some people are very aware of their "ethnicity." Some people might not even know it exists. People

Figure 8.5 Opening Ceremony Honoring Veterans with Flag and Staff Bearers Holding United States of America Flag, POW (Prisoners of War - Missing In Action during the Vietnam War) Flag, and Two Native American Staffs at the Annual Pow Wow Held at the Sunwatch Archaeological Site in Dayton, Ohio. June 22, 2019.
Source: Renée M. Bonzani.

can have identities that might be indigenous, ethnic, and national, all at the same time. One could be of the Cherokee indigenous group, ethnically identify as Native American, and consider oneself a U.S. citizen. Apparently, one might even identify with more than one ethnicity. As for instance, you might identify as Native American in some circumstances but also identify as American in another or as both at the same time (Figure 8.5), as clearly was the case of the code talkers; perhaps best known were the Navajo but they also included members of the Cherokee, Choctaw, Lakota, Meskwaki, Mohawk, Comanche, and Tlingit for the U.S. military during World Wars I and II. Sometimes one may not even identify with an ethnic group but one is placed in that group due to similarities in location, appearance, language, behaviors, and the like.

Ethnicity is like kinship in that people feel like kin through common descent but cannot trace the precise relationship (Maybury-Lewis, 2002:47). Ethnicity is also thought of as group identity based on its members' ideas of their own distinctiveness from others. Back to the concepts found in spatial-temporal territoriality, ethnicity is based on a sense of common history linked to a particular area or territory. It is a sense of relatedness that is ascribed to peoples, either by themselves or by others or both. These groups may or may not have a strong sense of common identity and they may or may not stick together. You can also identify as being part of a particular ethnic group but you can live many thousands of miles away from the homeland of that ethnic group.

The terms ethnicity and ethnic group are recent in origin with the use beginning in the 1940s and 1950s as a means to identify substate groups that were in conflict around the world. These groups were not political units of the state and the conflicts did not involve states fighting each other or at wars like in World War I and World War II. Instead, they were groups that could inhabit different states at the same time; or, within one state numerous of these groups were in conflict. These groups felt bound together by ties that lay between kinship and nationality (to be discussed below). Again, one can see the basic themes of spatial territory based on a temporal link to shared ancestors and the formation of large group categories as a means of differentiating between "us" and "them." Such notions can be seen as mechanisms of survival based on the idea that more security is found in larger number of people/animals.

Ethnicity then is thus activated when human beings are under stress. This leads us back to Darwin's first postulate or the notions of carrying capacity in that when there is economic stress or economic bad times, people will associate themselves to other groups of people who they perceive as being most like themselves. Ethnicity reflects a type of "kin", based on similar locations and past, even the past of a distant common homeland, sometimes referred to as "fatherland" or even "mother country." It is not uncommon for many immigrants and descendants even of the second or third generations to long to return to the homeland. Increased competition and a stress or lack of resources will cause people to fight for such resources; and, as one can envision, it is difficult to fight on your own but you would have a better chance of surviving if you are part of a group, let's say an ethnic group.

Ethnic groups can be indigenous groups such as the Sami who live along the Arctic Circle in parts of Scandinavia and even Russia. They are indigenous as being the first peoples in that area since time immemorial but they also identify as an ethnic group which can be particularly associated to whether you speak the language or not (Figure 8.6A and B).

Ethnic groups, however, do not have to be indigenous groups as the broad category "American" is sometimes utilized as an ethnic group to describe a people who live within the borders of the United States of America and who trace their founding fathers back to the War of Independence against the English monarchy, Declaration of Independence, and the writing of the Constitution of the United States of America. When I went to school, one felt a sense of unity or kinship with your other classmates as we pledged allegiance to the United States of America (Bellamy, 1892), as is done in elementary, middle, and high schools across the nation.

There can be many ethnic groups within a single state as well. Some might be minority ethnic groups with perhaps only a few thousand people who are also indigenous. On the other hand, one might belong to the majority ethnic group of a state like the Han Chinese that comprise hundreds of millions of people of similar ethnicity in modern China today (Figure 8.7).

Maybury-Lewis (2002: Chapter 2) gives numerous examples of ethnic groups around the world but to list just one other example he indicates that when the former Soviet Union existed, it contained from a Russian perspective a hierarchy of peoples. If you were Russian (as an ethnic group), you stood at the top of the hierarchy and were the elder brothers to all the rest and particularly to fellow Slavs from Ukraine and Belarus. These groups then felt themselves a cut above other Europeans within the Soviet Union like the Baltic peoples, Greeks, Moldavians, and people from the Caucasus. These groups then also distinguished themselves and felt superior to the large nationalities of Asiatic origin who also looked down on what we might call indigenous peoples. Indeed there is a Russian phrase that means "small-in-number peoples of the North" (Maybury-Lewis, 2002: 56). These indigenous peoples were transitory herders or hunter-gatherers of the far North and the term is still apparently used for small marginal societies within the larger state even in the South. In this example, we can see how identity can be formed to separate and also to build hierarchies which in essence can restrict the access to resources to only certain peoples and groups.

Figure 8.6A Three Sami Men in Finnish Lapland Wear Colorful Woolen Clothing. The Patterns on Their Jackets Are Largely Symbolic. Lapland, Finland. February 2, 2017.

Figure 8.6B Sami or Lappish Women in Traditional Clothes. Tromso, Norway. February 8, 2015.

Figure 8.7 Chinese Tourists, Many of Han Ethnicity, at Qing Dynasty Royal Palace Complex, Downtown Shenyang in Background, China. May 18, 2019.
Source: Renée M. Bonzani.

States

In the previous chapter, a definition of a state was given as a political unit that controls a usually large territory. A state is also defined as a single, supreme authority over a group of people occupying a common territory (Maybury-Lewis, 2002: Chapter 4). There are many aspects and characteristics of a state. Two of the most commonly cited are that the state is the agency or agencies within a society that have the monopoly over the legitimate use of violence. The state is also associated to a centralization of power.

An important key to remember is that the state is a political unit. It controls its own political decision-making process. It is an actual territorial unit. It is an autonomous unit that does not have a further overarching political entity to which it must answer. Even though the United Nations exists and makes conventions, an autonomous state can decide to follow the U.N. recommendations, or it can decide not to follow the U.N. recommendations.

On the other hand, in the United States of America, even though there are smaller political divisions referred to as states, these states and individuals within the U.S. borders must follow federal laws and policies passed in the capital of the United States by representatives of the people of the United States. Also, a state apparently has to be recognized as such by other states. It has to have developed institutions and policies which allow it to interact with other states on a somewhat heterarchical level. This means that each state has the equivalent recognized right to exist as such by all other states.

There are, of course, different kinds of states or, perhaps phrased more appropriately, different kinds of political structures that can arise and be found within a state. These include democracies, dictatorships, theocracies, and monarchies. As mentioned previously, there seems to be a rise around the world in the occurrence of democracies as the form of state government and this may be related to industrialization. In a democracy, the notion of individual free choice and equality are fundamental for the acceptance of the state. This view is based on the concept of society as a social contract which all individuals enter of their own free will (Rousseau, 1987 [1762]; Weber, 1930 [1904–1905, 1920]). States can also claim ownership over territories by utilizing the archaeological record to verify ancestral homelands; and, in some instances, by destroying the archaeological record, they can destroy the claim of others to the land.

Nations

If a nation has a different definition from a state, then what is a nation (Maybury-Lewis, 2002:108–109)? The nation is defined as a unit created by feelings of nationalism. Alright in school one is taught not to use the same words to give a definition; if a nation is defined by feelings of nationalism, then what is nationalism? Herein lies the difference between a state and a nation-state. Nationalism is the notion, emotion, or belief of a group occupying a particular territory that the nation and the state should coincide. When people within the territorial unit of the state, agree in belief, emotion and feelings that they belong to the state, then it is a nation-state. The feelings of nationalism for the state are at least somewhat shared by all or most individuals living within the territorial boundaries of that state.

Nationalism is the desire of individuals with common historical roots to control a particular territory. Sometimes this does happen (i.e., a nation-state) but sometimes the two do not coincide, so that one might find particular ethnic groups who have feelings of nationalism not for the state they are currently found in, but for one that they would like to have on their own. They want their own political autonomy. This desired territory may or may not be defined externally as a state.

A good example of this is found in present-day Iraq. Iraq is a state recognized by the United Nations and other states as having its own political structures and its own well-defined territory. However, within Iraq are numerous ethnic groups who have feelings of nationalism for their own state. These are peoples who perhaps feel like they do not have anything in common with the rest of the peoples in the state. They may feel left out of political decisions or do not share the same religion, language, or other practices as the majority groups in the state. The Kurds are an ethnic group whose members live in Iraq and Turkey in particular and in terms of nationalism, they are believed to want their own state, their own territory to control, and to live in without the influence of other people or ethnic groups that they do not feel close associations with.

Canada, closer here to the United States, is another example. Canada is a recognized state and its main political leaders are English speakers. However, within its borders there are ethnic and indigenous groups that feel a sense of nationalism that they would like to have their own state. These include First Nations peoples who have indigenous status and whose ancestors first arrived in the Americas potentially up to 25,000 years ago or earlier. They would like to have their own state. It also includes French-speaking Canadians who although they have not voted to try to establish their own state have voiced desires for this to happen, since they do not speak (or their primary language is not) English and they do not have the same historical backgrounds or cultures as the English speakers because their ancestors came from France and not England, for instance.

When nationalism, a strong commitment and sense of pride in the state and the boundaries of the political unit of the state coincide, one has a nation-state. Therefore, nationalism is also sometimes defined as strong feelings of commitment and attachment to one's own state above all other states. These feelings can be used to unify people particularly in times of stress or of threat to the state. The attack by the Japanese on Pearl Harbor in Hawaii helped foment feelings of nationalism in the United States which lead to its entering World War II in 1941, after internal conflicts in Europe and in eastern Asia had already been taking place (World War II from 1939–1945).

These feeling can also be used to isolate different states and they can be used to cause wars, wars to keep people out and wars to conquer/acquire new lands. The reasoning might be: one needs to start a war to acquire lands which should be part of the nation since our fellow countrymen and women are in these lands of a foreign power when they should be in the same nation-state as the rest of us. This appears to have been part of the mentality when Russia took over or annexed lands in Ukraine since fellow Russians lived there and they thought that they should actually be part of Russia. Access to the Black Sea and Sea of Azov probably also was a motivating factor (referred to as the Russo-Ukrainian War from 2014 to present).

Territoriality and feelings of nationalism can unify and can divide, can isolate peoples, or they can be used to promote ideas of inclusiveness. It seems to depend on the economic situation at the time and the history of each state as well as the actual people, actors, or agents involved.

Nation-building can also be used to motivate citizens to feel a sense of commitment to the state, rather than simply to their own peoples (tribes, ethnic groups) within the state. Examples of nation-building in the United States include the Fourth of July or Independence Day celebrations with fireworks, parades, picnics, etc., that are performed and have a unifying effect for people who call themselves Americans and celebrate July 4, 1776 and the beginnings of the Revolutionary War and independence and founding of the United States of America!

Maybury-Lewis (2002:121) indicates that these activities might be able to counteract tribalism which is the tendency for people to identify with their tribe primarily, if not exclusively, rather than with the state within which they live. This notion of tribalism is more common in countries or locations like Africa which have not undergone lengthy processes of industrialization and modernization which, as we have seen, tend to lead to the breaking down of larger kinship groups like clans that form tribes. A tribe is a territorial unit that can be formed through the unification of clans. In relation to the state, tribalism is a grouping together of marginal ethnic groups and indigenous peoples who still use their kinship relations to determine their place within a society and feel bound more-so with these groups than with the states within which they live. It is usually meant as a derogatory term in that the term is used to imply underdevelopment and lack of modernization or lack of the desire to modernize and fit in with the rest of the state's and world's views of how to live. These peoples feel that they do not have a stake in the state. They are not benefiting from the policies of the state; they do not have input into these policy-making decisions and would prefer to perhaps succeed from the state and form their own politically independent entity or just be left alone!

In this discussion, Maybury-Lewis brings up a dilemma in that democracies promote the well-being of the individual and in the long run have the goal of eliminating ethnicity (phrases like "one people under God" are utilized in the United States to promote this ideal). However, indigenous peoples in their demand for cultural survival are at odds with this notion. How can the state protect indigenous cultural identity or ethnic identity while still promoting the rights of all individuals? If ethnic or indigenous beliefs or rules endanger the individual or are at odds with other ethnic groups' beliefs within the state, which ethnic group and what practices would the state promote?

Figure 8.8 Children Riding Bicycles in Independence Day (4th of July) Parade and Carrying the Flag of the United States of America, **ca.** 1989.

Maybury-Lewis (2002: 128) brings up a good point when he discusses suggestions "that the state in multiethnic societies would have to defend collective as well as individual rights and, in effect, guarantee the circumstances under which ethnic groups can thrive." He counters this by stating, "The problem with such a guarantee is, as we have seen, that it involves the state in the business of protecting group rights rather than the individual rights that have been at the heart of enlightenment thinking about democracy and the social contract."

The United States of America is considered a nation-state. Feelings of nationalism are strong and a commitment to the state is well defined and promoted in different celebrations of the state including the Fourth of July, Veteran's Day, President's Day, and others when many people even can take the day off from work! On these days, the American flag is flown by people who identify themselves as Americans and who reside within the territorial boundaries of the United States of America or who associate with these territorial boundaries as their homeland, even if they are abroad (Figure 8.8).

Chapter 9

Globalization

Different Ways of Thinking about Economic Exchanges

Globalization from Above

Globalization can be understood as a world of things in motion. Images, objects, persons, and discourses all flow around the world in unprecedented ways that may not even have happened twenty years ago. Examples include the development of the internet and the ability to move ideas, faiths, and beliefs, and money across boundaries that never could have happened before this. People can move from one area of the world with modern transportation and be halfway around the globe in thirteen hours. Language apps allow people to go to a different part of the world and still be able to communicate.

Unfortunately, people can bring epidemics with them and/or intentionally or unintentionally transported plants and animals can do the same and the World Health Organization (WHO) and others are always on call trying to stop the spread of disease and epidemics. Terrorism and violence in one place can be incited by peoples with particular agendas who may never even have entered a country. In all of these examples, it seems to be that globalization can be seen as a means of opening up borders. It is a means of crossing what were traditional physical state, nation-state, and other sociopolitical boundaries by, in some way, circumventing those boundaries.

The potential reasons for globalization today, as well as in the past with, for instance, the explorations of the world in the 1400s and 1500s (Mann, 2006), appear to be economic in nature. Globalization then can be understood as a particular, contemporary configuration of the relationship between capital and nation-states whereby capital in this context is defined as money. The acquisition of money and ways to make money appear to be the driving force behind the globalization phenomenon and the linking of the world and its numerous states into a global telecoupled economy, as it is sometimes referred to (Ellis, 2015: 310). To understand this, one has to go back into a basic lesson that might be found in an economic anthropology class. In an Introduction to Anthropology class, one learns that economic exchanges can be studied in a number of different ways. Three of those include:

1. Formalist Approach.
2. Substantivist Approach.
3. Marxist Approach or Production Theory.

One of the anthropologists who developed the Formalist Approach to study economics was Melville Herskovits (1952, 1940). He was an American anthropologist who helped establish African and African-American studies at universities in the United States. He studied economic interactions through the neoclassical view of Adam Smith (1776) whereby rational action is the key to economic decisions. In other words, rational decision making should lead to a goal of the maximization of returns. One should want to maximize their return in any economic exchange.

In these market-based forms of exchange, the concepts of supply, demand, and price work together to make a type of equation that leads to numerous types of feedback loops (Figure 9.1). For instance, if the supply of something is low and demand stays the same, the price will increase. If we equate price with profit, we see that for a maximization of returns, we always want the profit to go up or to be high. One of the consequences of this is that demand needs to always increase: If supply stays the same and demand goes up, price and profit will go up. One can also note that if supply goes down or if there is the perception that the supply of something is scarce (even if it is not really) or is exclusive for only a certain set of people, then price and profit will go up.

In today's world of institutionalized businesses including banking, that is, the goal: The goal is a maximization of returns or more profit. Remember businesses are institutionalized forms of managing economic exchanges that are found in complex societies. Complex societies have functional differentiation and specialization in the different aspects or components of their societies. One of

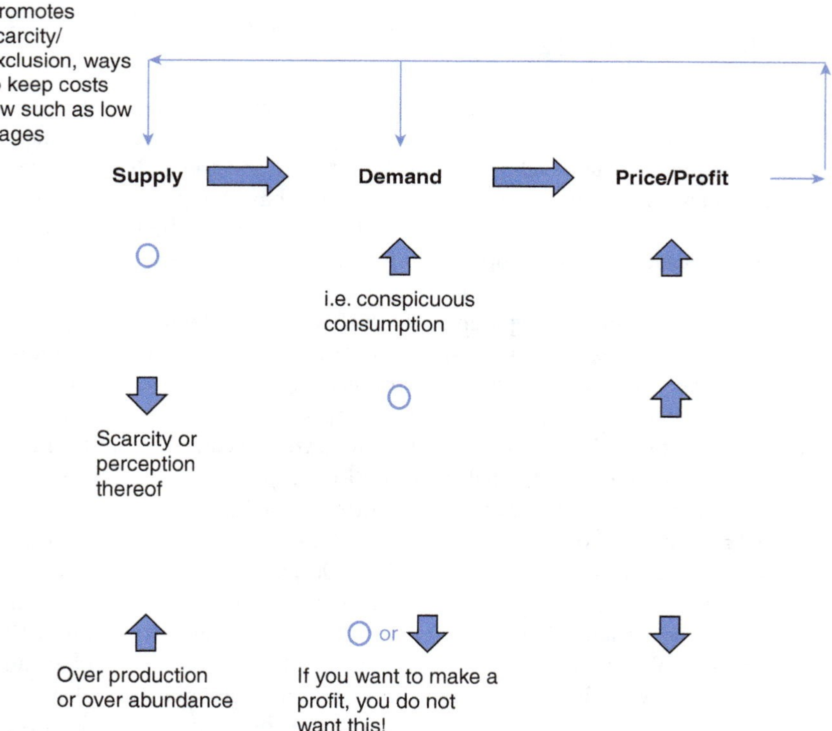

Figure 9.1 Market-Based Feedback Loops Based on the Relationship between Supply, Demand, and Price/Profit.

these components is related to economics which is defined as "a social science concerned chiefly with description and analysis of the production, distribution, and consumption of goods and services" (www.merriam-webster.com/dictionary/economics).

In complex societies institutions that manage economic exchanges become separated from other aspects of society: They are not religious entities whose specialized function of the individuals who work in them is to feel guilty about ripping someone off. They are not moral or political entities though they can influence and be influenced by these. The people who are CEOs of big businesses or banks are not religious leaders; nor are they political leaders; nor do they specialize and spend most of their time in teaching, medicine, law, etc. They specialize in making a profit. Indeed one can look at the film "The Business of America" (produced by California Newsreel in 1984) (Feinglass, 1984) and in it they interview the CEO of U.S. Steel at the time. Basically, the interviewer asks him what the goal of the steel business or industry is. One would expect him to say to make high-quality steel but he says that the goal of the business is to make a profit. Therefore, if one keeps that in mind, one can understand how globalization or the global world economic system works today.

Before this point is further explored, one should know that there are other approaches to studying economic interactions and these approaches recognize the fact that sometimes the goal of the exchange is not to make a profit but to build reciprocal relations. This second approach is called the Substantivist Approach and under this approach the economic anthropologist Marshall Sahlins and the economist Karl Polanyi are credited with making substantial contributions to this field of study. Marshall Sahlins is an American Anthropologist who wrote a well-known book called "Stone Age Economics" (1972) and worked with Pacific Island societies, specifically on Fiji and Hawaii. Karl Polanyi was a well-known economic historian whose publications include "The Great Transformation" (1944) where he basically noted that economic relations were greatly transformed after the advent of the Industrial Revolution in the late 1700s and 1800s.

In these books, these scholars indicate that not all economic exchanges in all societies are based on the profit motive. In fact, in nonindustrial societies at the time, they noted that exchanges can be based on reciprocity or the exchange of goods and services of equal value and done to build relations that can be sustained over time. They identified three types of exchanges including:

1. Generalized exchange whereby those who exchange things (goods, labor) do so without expecting an immediate return and the value of the return is also not specified. Marcel Mauss (1966 [1925]) also noted these types of exchanges in his well-known book called "The Gift: Forms and Functions of Exchange in Archaic Societies" whereby gift—giving is actually a form of building reciprocal relations (also see Malinowski, 1922). A gift is given; it is accepted; and at some point in the future the gift is expected to be returned.
2. Balanced exchange is like barter whereby exchange is done in equal terms or values. One exchanges something for something else that both parties consider are of equal value.
3. Negative exchange, then, seems to be what is being described in the Formalist Approach whereby the exchange that is being conducted is done so that one party seeks a profit in the relationship.

All three of these types of economic exchanges can appear in a society such as the United States where one can identify all three types as, for instance, when you help someone move (a form of labor exchange) and next year they help you; when you exchange a necklace you made for one of the scarfs your friend knitted and dyed; or when you run a small business and have to sell your cupcakes for more than they cost you to produce so that you can make a profit to keep your business running and so that you can go on vacation next summer.

The third approach, the Marxist Approach or Production Theory, has already been described in Chapter 7 under Stratified Societies and is used to describe large stratified societies that have classes whereby people are found in particular classes dependent upon whether or not they are the owners of the means of production. This approach studies the relationship of different classes of people based on the concepts of labor, means of production, and the modes of production and how in already complex, often industrial societies, the relationship between these factors can help to determine the type of political/economic system that is practiced in that society.

From these studies, then one knows that not everything has to be done to make a profit but not in the globalized world run by big businesses, that is the goal. Therefore, as stated, globalization can be understood as a particular, contemporary configuration in the relationship between capital and nation-states. Nation-states are large complex societies and the global capital or how to obtain capital on a global scale is characterized by strategies that involve predatory behaviors or predatory mobility, both across space and time. Governments, resources, peoples, and individuals are in essence seen as prey and utilized for extractive purposes with the main goal to make a profit, although such actions are often couched in terms of benefits to individuals such as to produce jobs (which they can, of course).

However as in hunting wild animals (Clutton-Brock, 1989), the relationship between predator and prey is temporary; long-term investment and the wealth and welfare of the peoples and individuals involved are not a primary goal or concern. These predatory behaviors and actions can be seen as being geared toward acquiring wealth from individuals and resources from states, nations, ethnic groups, and indigenous groups. The gold mining company or oil industry moves into an area to acquire the resources in that area. Once the resources are extracted, the company leaves. No continued investment is guaranteed; no continued jobs are guaranteed; no pension plans are guaranteed; no reimbursement for the extraction of resources is guaranteed; a clean environment is not guaranteed.

It is a strange, interesting, and wonderful country that we or, more personally, I live in being born and raised in the United States, a U.S. citizen who has spent most of her life here where we have CEOs who are professed American, U.S. citizens, vote Republican or Democrat or Independent, and who want a strong military yet will move their companies' factories to another country, so that they can pay lower wages to the workers there. Why do they do that? Isn't that anti-American? Well, given the above information it makes sense because they run businesses; again, they are not politicians; they are not military leaders; they are not religious community leaders (though they can be); they are primarily leaders of businesses whose goal is to make a profit. The business or corporation in the United States can legally be set up as a separate entity from the individuals who own them. In fact, that is probably what you want so that if your business gets sued for something, it will not affect your own personal assets. There appears to be no contradiction in these individuals' identities because one has become so functionally separated from the other that in the consciousness of Americans in general, there is no contradiction in these behaviors. The CEO of Fiat Chrysler (FCA) can decide to move some of the factory production to Mexico even though the company had previously accepted money from the U.S. government and people under Presidential support to stop the company from falling into bankruptcy (for instance see "The Detroit News," October 29, 2018).

Back in 1997, William Grieder (1997) noted that globalization is like a run-away horse without a rider. It is creating increases in inequality within societies and between societies (for instance, see the video on Wealth Inequality in America at www.youtube.com/watch?v5QPKKQnijnsM). Also there seems to be no doubt that the processes of globalization, often linked to industrialization, are creating and have created a spiraling process of ecological degradation. Go to Los Angeles on a smoggy day and you will see why one should be thankful that Eugene Houdry, a French mechanical engineer and expert in catalytic oil refining, invented the catalytic converter for internal combustion engines found in automobiles, probably the individual's true emblem of living in an industrialized world. China today is perhaps only twenty years into their Industrial Revolution and already cities in China have major problems with air pollution due to running automobiles and machines and factories and the use of nonrenewable fuel sources that are major pollutants to the atmosphere. The list of clear ecological/environmental degradation around the world today can go on and on.

Researchers on this issue also go back to big business and the profit motive to indicate that there is an unviable relationship between finance and manufacturing capital. This is a complicated topic but what seems to happen is that when a manufacturing factory is doing well, all is good: The company is making a profit and people have jobs, benefits, and pensions. However, as machines get old and need to be updated and technologies change, it takes investments by the owners to improve these aspects of the business as well as to train workers. This reinvestment often does not happen and the case of the aging steel mills in Pittsburgh in the 1970s and 1980s are a case in point. Almost all of

Figure 9.2 Advertisement Promoting their Product BEL-AIR No. 8.
©Mike Clarke/Staff/Getty Images

these mills were eventually shut down due to a lack of reinvestment to update aging machinery and antiquated technologies.

What seems to happen is that for large multinational companies or corporations that can move investments and money around instead of worrying about actual places and peoples, the question becomes why invest in a dying or degrading manufacturing factory in one location of the United States or world when you can move the money from profits or tax breaks into banking or finance or some other industry and location and make more money without reinvesting? Again there is no business morality tied into the fact that many of these people will lose their jobs, livelihoods, homes, pensions. Yet new industries, new jobs, new technologies in new locations can arise based on this influx of money, that is one of the reasons that this is such a complicated issue. However apparently, finance and manufacturing capital are not one in the same thing, or maybe it is more like the saying "you cannot be in two places at the same time."

For individuals, everyone knows how big businesses get our money. I see a commercial or advertisement and I really want to be like the person in the add (Figure 9.2). Subliminal messages in advertisements have made many feel that if they buy the product, they will become part of the group and this fits perfectly with the neoclassical view of economic exchanges because demand for a product has to remain high or increase for prices and profits to rise, which is exactly what you want. You want demand to increase. Conspicuous consumption, a concept developed by Thorstein Veblen in a book called "The Theory of the Leisure Class" (1899), is the term that refers to the fact that in certain circumstances material goods are consumed because they give prestige or status, not because they are necessary. We become part of a group if we can look, act, behave, and buy and own the same things that the group owns. This behavior often is found in groups or classes of a society that have expendable income (income not needed for the basic necessities of life) or one might add, borrowed income. The promotion of this type of status- or prestige-seeking behavior and spending habits adds to demand and consumerism that is promoted around the world today. The flashing advertisements on the side of your webpage, cell phone, interruptions on TV, and constant barrage of adds everywhere is testimony to the globalized profit-oriented class of institutionalized big business.

Are there any potential benefits to all of this? Well, there must be or people in the United States and elsewhere in the world would probably not continue to follow along these lines of living, though perhaps an awakening of consciousness is again taking place whereby people look at their own actions of consumption and have become more ecologically and environmentally conscious, at least in many parts of the United States. Here in the United States, for instance, recycling is definitely more common than it was in the 1970s when basically no one or very few people recycled anything at the household level like aluminum cans. Even in China the notion of recycling and care of the environment can be found (Figure 9.3).

Figure 9.3 Illustration of Recycling Efforts and Environmentalism in China
©Al.geba/Shutterstock.com

Perhaps we are all looking for progress or the idea of progress that is defined as the development of an individual or society in a direction considered to be more beneficial than and superior to the previous level or condition.

Besides issues related to the globalized economic system based off of the goal to make a profit and the problems of inequality and environmental degradation that are occurring, we see that issues related to immigration have more than ever taken center stage on the news in relation to problems faced by numerous people who have to or want to move and those into whose territories they are moving. Indeed, in a U.S. Today Special Report in 2015 the headline read: "Record Refugee Flights Hit All Parts of the Globe" and "Number Forced from Homes could Hit 55 Million This Year". An accompanying graph shows that refugee immigration has increased from 19.5 million in 2004 to 54.9 million in 2014, a 35.5 percent increase in only ten years! What is happening?

Migration has been and is a basic aspect of human adaptations. There are three well-researched phases of human migration in prehistory and a fourth in historic times. This information comes from an interesting book by Peter Bellwood (2013, also see his book published in 2005) in which he outlines the different phases of prehuman and human migration through time with much of the data on this coming from archaeological and linguistic evidence. These phases include the following:

1. Migrations of the extinct members of the genus *Homo,* such as *Homo erectus* and Neanderthals, after about 2.5 million years ago, within and out of Africa.
2. Migrations of ancestral modern humans (*Homo sapiens*) throughout most of the world including Australia and the Americas, between about 120,000 and 25,000 years ago.
3. Migrations of herders, farmers, and boat builders in a number of separate waves in various parts of the world except Antarctica during the last 10,000 years.
4. The fourth historic migration phase or "diaspora" involved ca. 150 million people in three waves peaking in the 1840s and the 1950s. One wave went from western Europe to the Americas and Australasia. Another went from India and China to the Indian Ocean rim, Southeast Asia, and the South Pacific. A third migration went from Russia and China into central and northeastern Asia.

Humans are generally mobile; they move around a lot. When looking at larger-scale mobility, current terms to keep in mind include:

Immigration = the movement of nonnative people into a country in order to settle there.

Emigration = the act of or instance of emigrating or to more away, to depart from a place. To leave a place or country, especially one's native country, in order to settle in another.

Diaspora = any group migration or flight from a country or region; any group that has been dispersed outside of its traditional homeland, especially involuntarily.

Refugee = one that flees; especially a person who flees to a foreign country or power to escape danger or persecution.

(Definitions from http://dictionary.reference.com and https://www.merriam-webster.com/dictionary/)

Bellwood (2013: 5) notes: "But, in my view, the real energy behind the world's major colonizing migrations was human and demographic, in the sense that increasing human populations required new resources, especially territory, and more so if other groups or declining environmental conditions impinged on a long-term basis on the territories they already held." As human populations reach unprecedented levels at 7,578,217,500 billion as of 4:44 p.m. EST on June 12, 2019 (www.census.gov/popclock/), we can expect migrations of people to continue and increase as resource limitations are reached, as the climate changes, as war and disease affect different areas, as people push and move into different territories already occupied by others.

Reasons for immigration include drought, flooding, earthquakes, volcanic eruptions, epidemics, need for work, need for labor including slavery, need for land (population density), warfare (refugees), illegal drug trade retaliations (refugees), ideological/religious or other persecution (refugees).

In the United States migration is nothing new. In fact in a book by Colin Woodard (2011) called "American Nations," he identifies eleven rival regional cultures or "nations" as he calls them in North America. These eleven locations have defined borders and cultural practices that differ between them. The borders and territories do not correspond to existing state boundaries in the United States, Canada, or Mexico and he outlines how these locations and differences in beliefs, behaviors, languages, and other cultural manifestations can be traced back to migrations from different parts of mainly Europe to different parts of the United States in the 1600s, 1700s, 1800s, and early 1900s. This review is an interesting study that can help us understand local differences in cultural practices, languages, foods, dress, and beliefs within North America in general.

Through the use of ethnographies and comparing changes that have occurred in some societies around the world, one can see that indeed globalization and modernization can be both a blessing and a curse. The consequences of these globalized, now telecoupled through global telecommunication networks, interactions can be both problematic or progressive (progress) depending upon who one talks to. For example, in the ethnography by Karl G. Heider (1970) entitled "The Dugum Dani. A Papuan Culture in the Highlands of West New Guinea" and the film "Dead Birds" (Parts I, II, and III, recorded in the Grand Valley of the Baliem, western mountains of West New Guinea in 1962, produced by Robert Gardner with Harvard University), one is presented with autonomous political groups (confederations and sibs) that practiced intensive horticulture and had well-defined territorial units protected by watchtowers where men would watch for enemies crossing no-man's-lands. A stylized form of warfare or ritualized feuding would at times result in the death of a relative leading to a cycle of revenge whereby the ghost (*mogat* which appears to come from a soul-like entity, the *akotakun*) of the dead person had to be avenged for honor and fear of the dead person's ghost and how it might affect the "soul" (*edai-egen* literally translated as "seed of singing") of the living relatives (Heider, 1970: 226—227). After 1963 Indonesia with Dutch colonial influence annexed that part of New Guinea and it became known at Irian Jaya until 2007 and is now a province of Indonesia called West Papua.

A later film made in 1992 entitled "Arrows against the Wind" (produced by Tracey Groome for Bullfrog Films) recorded the consequences of annexation, globalization, and enculturation to the Dani and other indigenous groups in West New Guinea. The negative effects of these processes, the predatory economic policies, and issues with immigration and transmigration are revealed. The political structure of the Dani is basically destroyed; male power, position, and status and the previous territorial delineation of different political entities appears to have been subjugated; territorial control of land of other indigenous groups is lost to transmigrants from other areas of Indonesia done to reduce overcrowding and overpopulation in these other locations; economic labor exploitation of other indigenous groups is obvious; collusion between government military commanders and multinational big businesses and corporations is noted; and environmental degradation is secretly filmed by plane above a multinationally run mineral mine. By reading the ethnographies and watching these different films, a list of issues viewed as problems versus progress is possible. For now, this brief list follows:

Problems	versus	Progress
• Deforestation	——-	New and continued supply of forest products.
• Loss of indigenous territories	——-	Transmigration, new land for peoples from over-populated areas.
• Local need for money and jobs	——	Free trade and access to industrialized goods.
• Cash crops and loss of diversity	——	Increase production of crops in world demand.
• Loss of local cultural practices	——	One culture/language and media access.
• Debt	——	Profit/wealth to owners of the means of production including middlemen and money lenders.

Each of these can be seen as a problem that at the local level indigenous and other ethnic groups have had to deal with. However, at a global level these same local problems might relieve population pressure somewhere else or they might supply goods that are in limited supply on the world market elsewhere. Modernization and technological innovations may become accessible as would transportation, telecommunications, electricity, and access to other resources like bank loans to build local businesses and schools and hospitals. These situations are like two sides of the same coin or as in the United States one might hear a "Catch-22," defined as a dilemma or difficult circumstance from which there is no escape because of mutually conflicting or dependent conditions (www.google.com) and coined from the title of a satirical novel by American author Joseph Heller (1961). At the local level, how might people deal with these issues?

Globalization from Below

Here only a few examples of how people might deal with these global issues are given and include the formation of cooperatives and the use of NGOs (nongovernmental organizations) that help local, indigenous, and ethnic groups deal with various of these issues. Cooperatives are groups of people usually from the same region and ethnic groups or even the same kinship group that maintain control each over their own resources, land, products but unite to take advantage of economic niches where they can offer their resources or products in bulk so that they can contend more so with global price changes and competition. Cooperatives are seen as larger units of cooperating individuals and their families that can deal with global economic effects better than could an individual and his/her family alone.

Cooperatives, then, can be defined as economic structures whereby individuals of similar backgrounds, ethnicity, etc., group together to contend with larger-scale economic forces beyond their control. Many examples exist such as coffee cooperatives in Central America or your local grocery store cooperative that you can join as a member and then can participate as a supplier, buyer, and owner all at the same time. Indeed in 2012, the United Nations named that the "Year of Cooperatives" to honor the use of cooperative organizations to contribute to socioeconomic development across the world (www.un.org/en/events/coopsyear/).

The second example of NGOs also help at the local level and work with public officials, international civil societies' organizations, and different local organizations. They often work with lawyers to help develop protections for local peoples in terms of land deeds and other legal issues and contracts. They can work on voting rights, civil rights, and issues related to the environment.

As reviewed in Chapter 4, there is a trend toward individualism in the world today and toward the protection of the individual in global legal relations as interactions between different ethnic groups, states, nation-states, and global predatory business practices manifest into numerous forms of conflict. In response the world community has developed legal recourse through the Universal Declaration of Human Rights (adopted by the United Nations on December 10 of 1948) (www.un.org/en/universal-declaration-human-rights/) and the International Covenant on Civil and Political Rights (adopted by the United Nations on December 19 of 1966) (//treaties.un.org/doc/publication/unts/volume%20999/volume-999-i-14668-english.pdf). Universal education for all is perhaps one of the most important initiatives on the global world agenda for the protection of individual human rights (for instance through UNESCO, the United Nation's Educational, Scientific, and Cultural Organization).

Living in an individualized globalized world that we do, many want to affect the world through individual actions that must take into account cultural and material, social and political, and ecological and environmental aspects of the world that can lead to progress. For the future generations, these are all inheritances that we will leave for those that come after us.

Epilogue

Where Are We Going? The Anthropocene and Genetic, Cultural/Material, Social/Political, and Ecological/Environmental Inheritances

The last chapter is probably the most opinionated of all of the chapters as I have tried to stick to the definitions and concepts as found in these different topics covered in Anthropology. However, globalization takes us into the future and no one really knows what might happen. We do have some clues though; so, finally, I just want to mention the concept of the "Anthropocene" and briefly summarize this concept and the different ways it might let us predict what might happen in the future and the different aspects of human societies and their relationships to the landscapes and environments that we find ourselves in.

Erle C. Ellis (2018) recently wrote a short concise book entitled "Anthropocene. A Very Short Introduction" (also see Ellis et al., 2018). In this book he explains humans' effects on the landscape and environment beginning with advent of agriculture at about 10,000 years ago and continuing into the industrial era and the age of radioactivity. He indicates that many scholars would like to make this time period, though the beginning point is debated, into a new geological era, that of the Anthropocene. He gives various forms of information and graphs that indicate from hard data that humans have changed the landscape and the environment in innumerable ways and that the current issues related to climate change and the warming of the Earth are founded in scientific fact.

Whether the warming of the earth is part of a "natural" cyclic change of climate or whether it is human induced still seems to be up to debate. Archaeologically, we know that major cycles of warming and/or drought have occurred in South American Andean prehistory at ca. 900–700 BCE, 560–590 CE, and again at 1000–1200 CE (Burger, 1992; Kolata and Ortloff, 1996; Moseley, 2001; Shimada et al., 1991). In Mesoamerica, events of major drought and climate change are some of the possible explanations for the collapse of the lowland Maya city states at ca. 800–900 CE (Coe, 1993; Coe and Koontz, 2002; Price and Burton, 2011: 198; Price and Feinman, 2008: 322; Sharer, 1994). In North America, climate change which may have involved flooding and then tree-ring-recorded droughts with the first recorded at 1288–1308 CE is given as part of the reason for the collapse of Cahokia and its Mississippian cultural influences beginning around ca. 1150–1250 CE (Meeks and Anderson, 2013; Pauketat and Emerson, 1997).

Climate change then is nothing new. However, the scale of the change in temperature warming and the influence of humans in relation to raising carbon dioxide (CO_2), nitrous oxide (N_2O), other greenhouse gases, and radioactivity is unprecedented since the turn of the last century (1900s).

Just this last May, I had the great honor to be able to teach, through a Faculty teaching program between the Confucius Institute at the University of Kentucky and Jilin University in Changchun, China, a course on the "Origins of New World Civilizations." I asked my Chinese undergraduate students to read over sections of this book and answer a few questions on a work sheet. I thought it was important to see what people actually think about these issues and especially young undergraduate students who have most of their lives still ahead of them and who will have to deal with many of these issues related to climate change and global warming. I hope to do this with my U.S. students also but here are just a few paraphrased or quoted examples of what they said.

What is met by the "Anthropocene"?

The Anthropocene is being proposed as a new interval of geological time. Since humans have changed the world so greatly, some experts separate this age with human influence from the Holocene.

On the other hand, "The Anthropocene is more about pop culture than hard science. The Anthropocene provides eye catching jargon, but from the geological side."

Have carbon dioxide levels been increasing through time? Give an example of how this is shown scientifically.

"Yes. In the prehistoric period, CO_2 levels are sometimes high and sometimes low like a loop but after the industrial revolution, the CO_2 levels keep increasing more than in past time periods." This is from Ellis (2018: 23).

The Keeling Curve (Ellis 2018: 25) details changes to CO_2 since 1960. Carbon dioxide has increased steeply across the last century, rising to levels unprecedented across the entire Holocene.

Long-term surveys have found that Kilimanjaro's snow line is rising.

Based on ice-core records from Antarctica, which can indicate the changes in carbon dioxide and climate.

Sea level rises.

How have humans added to the amount of carbon dioxide in the atmosphere?

Mass combustion of fossil fuels was in fact causing carbon dioxide to accumulate in the earth's atmosphere.

Combustion of organic matter (coal, methane, gas, gasoline, etc.).

The Industrial Revolution has resulted in widespread land clearing for agriculture, causing release of carbon dioxide, and potentially global climate change.

The production of steel and cement. The deposits of plastics. Cutting down trees/reduction of green environment. The exhaust from cars and factories. Increase in meat consumption. Increasing populations.

List at least five ways humans have changed nature and the environment/landscape.

1. Anthropomorphic landscapes are generally mosaics of used lands interspersed with less used recovering and remnant ecosystems.
2. Engineered soils.
3. Managed vegetation including the indigenous societies that had long cultivated crops and used fire to manage their vegetation.
4. Excess nutrients.
5. Pollution.
6. Other human-altered conditions.
7. Polluting the oceans with fertilizer run-off from agriculture.
8. Transforming natural habitats around the world.
9. Freshwater appropriations have long increased with population and food demand.
10. Hunting and foraging pressures generally increased.
11. Emissions of nitrous oxide from fertilized fields are increasing in Earth's atmosphere.

The list goes on…

List at least five areas in the world where agriculture first began.

1. Southwest Asia.
2. South America.
3. North China.
4. Yangtze China.
5. Central America and Mexico.

This list also included other areas for the origins of food production.

What is the pristine myth?

"The pristine myth: that places without humans today represents an ecology without prior human influence. This myth is now recognized as a serious barrier to understanding contemporary ecological patterns and processes."

Some students tied this to mythology and the origin cosmologies of Christianity or to fairy tales of magical and supernatural beings and lands:

"The Jewish old testament and the Christian Bible contain two mythic origin stories that are accepted by modern Judaism and Christianity. In the first fairy tale, God says, "let the light shine here!" Then light appeared, and in six days God made the sky, the land, the planets, the sun, and the moon, including all the animals of man. On the seventh day God rested and looked at his work with great satisfaction. In the second fairy tale, God created the first man on earth, Adam. God created an Eden for Adam to live in a carefree life, but forbade him to eat the fruit of the Eden tree, which came from the tree of good and evil consciousness. Adam's life was so lonely that God took a rib from Adam's body and created the first woman—Eve. A talking serpent tempted Eve to eat the forbidden fruits. Then Eve persuaded Adam to eat the forbidden fruit. When God discovered this, he expelled Adam and Eve from the Garden of Eden and made them mortal."

Do you think human population growth has or will reach a level on earth when that level can no longer be sustained by the existing resources? Why or Why not?

"I don't think the population will reach that level, because populations are limited by scarce resources of natural selection. Earth's human populations are continuing to urbanize and population growth rates are continuing to drop."

On the other hand, "I think population will reach a level due to limited resources. Though population growth is slowing, human demands for food, water, energy, and other environmental resources are continuing to grow, as wealthier populations make greater demands on Earth's resources. Moreover, many scientists and others are concerned that even current levels of population and resource demand may be harming Earth's life support systems in ways that might prove catastrophic in the future."

Do you think that the text that you read makes some good points about humans' effect on climate change? Why or why not?

"Yes. Firstly, the text connects the trend of climate change with the outlines of humans' activities through time by means of scientific statistic analysis of data, which is very convincing. Secondly, we can read some examples and comparations from the true condition, which can reflect the dependency between the humans' activity and climate change. Thirdly, the text states the facts and opinions from an objective perspective, which can enhance reliability of it. So considering the three aspects above, I think the text really makes some good points and the methods and logic way of thinking is worth using for reference."

Do you think a new geological time period should be named the "Anthropocene"? Why or why not?

"No. The Earth is a natural system which has been running for billions of years. And we human beings are just a species living in a short time interval, though we reshaped the Earth in the past thousands of years, but we do not take control of the Earth. We just make a living by using the resources of the Earth. So we are weaker than the nature like earthquake, flood, hurricane, and so on. Although we reshaped the earth, the natural environment can recover and change automatically decades or years without human's activity. So, we should not define a new geological time period as 'Anthropocene.'"

On the other hand, "Yes. I do. Humanity's impact upon planet Earth is now so profound that we are about to be recognized as a geological force of nature. We settled down, organized into civilizations, and embarked on the explosion of population, industrialization, and technology that has precipitated planetary changes. All this has earmarks of a geological transition."

Define in class what the following terms might mean: genetic inheritance, cultural inheritance, social (political) inheritance, and ecological/environmental inheritance.

Just one of many good answers:

"Genetic inheritance is a kind of inheritance about physical characteristics, such as the shape of head and skull, color of eyes, the proportion of each part in the whole body, and so on. We can view it as the result of evolution both in heredity and variation.

Cultural inheritance is a kind of inheritance both tangible form and intangible form. The tangible form is the material legacy from our ancestors, such as the Great Wall, the Pyramid, and so on. The intangible cultural inheritance is about some crafts or skills, some kinds of art, and so on. The cultural inheritance is the symbol of ancient people's intelligence and craftsmanship.

Social or political inheritance is about institution and law which was made by ancient people, and we can learn a lot from them, such as Hammurabi's code, centralism of ancient China, and so on. We use them for reference to our modern society.

Ecological or environmental inheritance is a kind of legacy which include the natural landscape, sustainable environment, and so on. Also, the resource can be included. We should preserve the sustainable environment and deliver to the next generation as the ecological inheritance."

Well, what do you as readers and other students think about these responses?

If one returns to the Substantivist Approach to economic analysis which includes preindustrial societies, this approach and the identified categories of exchange seem to be very similar to that taken by Descola (1994 [1986]) and Reichel-Dolmatoff (1976, 1997; also see Pálsson, 1996) and utilized in Oyuela-Caycedo (2004) when discussing how Amazonian indigenous groups interact with nature and the environment. One has to remember that many of these societies have a belief in animism or spirit entities that pervade and affect the landscape, environment, and outcome of events. In these relations, they identity three categories: predation where the relationship is seen as one of capturing and taking the desired resources; reciprocity where exchanges are made with nature and spirit entities (or even a God) and other humans to maintain a balance between humans and nature; and protection or a domestication relationship where humans are seen as the caretakers or protectors of the environment and which is associated to the use of domesticated plants and animals that are purposefully planted, cared for, fed, and bred with the final result being that the resource is utilized to maintain humans. Here again we are seeing different ways to approach economic interactions and nature and the environment, all of which have as ultimate goals the maintenance and perpetuation of the society or group under question.

As we move into a more and more controlled domesticated landscape manipulated by humans as indicated by Ellis in his book on the "Anthropocene" (2018) and others in relation to niche-construction theory (Odling-Smee et al., 2013, 2003; Odling-Smee and Laland, 2012; Laland et al., 1999; Smith, 2007a, 2007b, 2012; Zeder 2012) and the "Extended Evolutionary Theory" (Bonduriansky and Day, 2009; Danchin et al., 2011; Mesoudi et al., 2006, 2004), perhaps a potential lesson is to begin to view nature and other people not as prey but in a reciprocal manner or at least in terms of the environment in a manner of stewardship or caretakers. I do not include humans in this last category as this verges on racism and is reminiscent of the excuses often given by colonial powers for their control over other societies in that they were caretakers since the other society's members could not take care of themselves or needed guidance in following the correct/civilized way to do things.

What a complicated world we live in but we can start to think of options for economic relations and the globalized world which are not just extractive, negative exchange mechanisms that leave some people and societies impoverished, landscapes for humans and nonhumans destroyed, and that do not take into consideration future genetic, cultural, social, and environmental inheritances or consequences of these actions. Surely, humans are smarter than that. We may not be able to predict exactly what will happen in the future, but we can use our powers of observation and past histories and prehistories to help guide us toward futures that we want, that are sustainable, that indicate "progress," and that perhaps will lead to new formations of "imagined communities."

Bibliography

Aiyar, Mani Shankar. "Secularism, Atheism, Agnosticism." *India International Centre Quarterly* 35, no. 2 (2008): 122–35.

Allen, John L., and Audrey C. Shalinsky. *Student Atlas of Anthropology.* New York: McGraw-Hill Companies, 2004.

Anderson, Benedict. *Imagined Communities: Reflections on the Origin and Spread of Nationalism.* London: Verso, 1983.

"Anthropology." In *Dictionary.* Accessed March 31, 2019. www.dictionary.com/browse/anthropology.

Barth, Fredrik. *Ethnic Groups and Boundaries.* Boston: Little Brown, 1969.

Becerra, Gabriel Cabrera, Carlos Eduardo Franky Calvo, and Dany Mahecha Rubio. *Los Nukak: Nómadas de la Amazonía Colombiana.* Bogotá, Editorial Universidad Nacional, 1999.

Bellamy, Francis. "The Pledge of Allegiance." In *The Youth's Companion.* 1892. http://www.ushistory.org/documents/pledge.htm.

Bellwood, Peter. *First Migrants: Ancient Migration in Global Perspective.* Malden, MA: Wiley, Blackwell, 2013.

————. *First Farmers: The Origins of Agricultural Societies.* Maldin, MA: Blackwell Publishing, 2005.

Boas, Franz. *Race, Language, and Culture.* New York: The Macmillan Company, 1940.

————. *The Mind of Primitive Man,* revised ed. New York: Macmillan, 1938 [1911].

Bonduriansky, R., and T. Day. "Nongenetic Inheritance and Its Evolutionary Implications." *Annual Review of Ecology, Evolution, and Systematics* 40 (2009): 103–25.

Bonzani, Renèe M. *Bare Backbones: A Brief Introduction to Anthropology.* Cognella, Inc., 2016.

————. "Seasonality, Predictability and Plant Use Strategies at San Jacinto 1, Northern Colombia." PhD diss., Department of Anthropology, University of Pittsburgh, 1995.

————. "Territorial Boundaries, Buffer Zones, and Socio-Political Complexity: A Case Study of the Nuraghi on the Island of Sardinia." In *Sardinia in the Mediterranean: A Footprint in the Sea: Studies in Sardinian Archaeology Presented to Miriam S. Balmuth,* Monographs in Mediterranean Archaeology 3, edited by Robert H. Tykot and Tamsey K. Andrews. Sheffield, Sheffield Academic Press, 1992, 210–20.

Boserup, Ester. *The Conditions of Agricultural Growth; the Economics of Agrarian Change under Population Pressure.* Chicago: Aldine Pub, 1966.

Braudel, Fernand. *The Structures of Everyday Life: Civilization & Capitalism 15th–18th Century,* vol. 1. New York: Harper & Row Publishers, 1981 [1979].

Burger, R. *Chavin and the Origins of Andean Civilization.* London: Thames and Hudson, 1992.

Carmichael, Patrick H. "Nasca Burial Patterns: Social Structure and Mortuary Ideology." In *Tombs for the Living: Andean Mortuary Practices,* edited by Tom D. Dillehay. Washington, DC: Dumbarton Oaks Research Library and Collection, 1995.

Cashdan, Elizabeth. "Territoriality among Human Foragers: Ecological Models and an Application to Four Bushman Groups." *Current Anthropology* 24, no. 1 (1983): 47–66.

————. "Effects of Food Production on Mobility in the Central Kalahari." In *From Hunters to Farmers,* edited by J. Desmond Clark and Steven A. Brandt, 311–27. Berkeley: University of California Press, 1984.

————.*Risk and Uncertainty in Tribal and Peasant Economies.* Boulder, CO: Westview Press, 1990a.

————. "Introduction." In *Risk and Uncertainty in Tribal and Peasant Economies*, edited by Elizabeth Cashdan, 1–16. Boulder, CO: Westview Press, 1990b.

————. "Spatial Organization and Habitat Use." In *Evolutionary Ecology and Human Behavior,* edited by Eric Alden Smith and Bruce Winterhalder, 237–66. New York, NY: Aldine de Gruyter, 1992.

"Catch-22." In *Google Dictionary.* Accessed June 13, 2019. (www.google.com/search?rlz51C1CHFX_enUS705US705&ei5HGkCXcS-N–W_QaTm6rQDw&q5catch122&oq5catch122&gs_l5psy-ab.3..0l5j0i131j0l4.7518669.7521049..7522068...0.0..0.214.1003.3j4j1......0....1..gws-wiz.......0i67j35i39.HLOzSN9-0Rk)

Chagnon, Napoleon A. *Yanomamö: The Fierce People,* 3rd ed. New York: Holt, Rinehart, and Winston, 1983.

Charbit, Yves, and SpringerLink. *Economic, Social and Demographic Thought in the XIXth Century: The Population Debate from Malthus to Marx.* Dordrecht: Springer, 2009.

Clark, J. E., and M. Blake. "The Power of Prestige: Competitive Generosity and the Emergence of Rank in Lowland Mesoamerica." In *Factional Competition and Political Development in the New World,* edited by E. M. Brumfiel and J. W. Fox, 17–30. Cambridge: Cambridge University Press, 1994.

Clutton-Brock, Juliet, ed. *The Walking Larder: Patterns of Domestication, Pastoralism, and Predation.* London: Unwin Hyman, 1989.

Coe, Michael D. *The Maya.* New York: Thames & Hudson, 1993.

Coe, Michael D., and Rex Koontz. *Mexico: From the Olmecs to the Aztecs.* New York: Thames & Hudson, 2002.

Collateral Relatives. Accessed June 8, 2019. http://groups.molbiosci.northwestern.edu; http://groups.molbiosci.northwestern.edu/holmgren/Glossary/Definitions/Def-C/collateral_relatives.html.

College Tuition, College Board. Accessed May 9, 2019. https://www.collegedata.com/en/pay-your-way/college-sticker-shock/how-much-does-college-cost/whats-the-price-tag-for-a-college-education/.

"Confederation." In vocabulary.com. Accessed June 7, 2019. https://www.vocabulary.com/dictionary/confederation.

Danchin, E., A. Charmantier, F. A. Champagne, A. Mesoudi, B. Pujol, and S. Blanchet. "Beyond DNA: Integrating Inclusive Inheritance into an Extended Theory of Evolution." *Nature Reviews Genetics* 12 (2011): 45–486.

Darwin, Charles. *On the Origin of Species by Means of Natural Selection, or the Preservation of Favoured Races in the Struggle for Life.* London: John Murray, 1859.

De Waal, Alex. "Genocide in Rwanda." *Anthropology Today* 10, no. 3 (1994): 1–2.

Definitions. In *Google.* Accessed May 8, 2019. https://www.google.com/search?q5definition1rationalim&rlz51C1CHFX_enUS705US705&oq5definition1rationalim&aqs5chrome..69i57j0l5.4385j1j7&sourceid5chrome&ie5UTF-8.

Definitions. In *Merriam-Webster.* Accessed May 8, 2019. https://www.merriam-webster.com/dictionary/magic.

Denevan, W. *The Native Population of the Americas in 1492.* Madison: University of Wisconsin Press, 1976.

Denitch, Bogdan. *Ethic Nationalism: The Tragic Death of Yugoslavia.* Cambridge, MA: University of Minnesota Press, 1994.

Descola, Phillipe. *The Spears of Twilight: Life and Death in the Amazon Jungle.* Translated from French by Janet Lloyd. London: Harper Collins Publishers, 1996 [1993].

————. *In the Society of Nature: A Native Ecology in Amazonia.* Translated from French by Nora Scott. Cambridge: Cambridge University Press, 1994 [1986].

Diamond, Jared M. *Guns, Germs, and Steel: The Fates of Human Societies.* New York: Norton, 2005.

Djilas, Aleksa. *The Contested Country: Yugoslav Unity and Communist Revolution, 1919-1953.* Cambridge, MA: Harvard University Press, 1991.

Dumont, Louis. *Homo Hierarchicus. The Caste System and Its Implications.* Chicago: The University of Chicago Press, 1970.

Durkheim, Emile. *The Division of Labor in Society.* Glencoe, IL: Free Press, 1947 [1893].

"Economics." In *Merriam-Webster.* Accessed June 12, 2019. www.merriam-webster.com/dictionary/economics.

Eliade, Mircea. *The Forbidden Forest.* Indiana: University of Notre Dame Press, 1978.

————. *Images et Symboles: Essais sur Symbolisme Magico-Religieux.* Paris: Gallimard, 1952.

Ellis, Erle C. *Anthropocene: A Very Short Introduction.* Oxford: Oxford University Press, 2018.

————. "Ecology in an Anthropogenic Biosphere." *Ecological Monographs* 85, no. 3 (2015): 287–31.

Ellis, Erle C., Nicholas R. Magliocca, Chris J. Stevens, and Dorian Q. Fuller. "Evolving the Anthropocene: linking multi-level selection with long-term social-ecological change." *Sustainability Science* 13 (2018): 119–28.

Evans-Pritchard, Edward Evan. *The Nuer: A Description of the Modes of Livelihood and Political Institutions of a Nilotic People*. Oxford: Clarendon Press, 1940.

Feinglass, Joe. "Film Review: The Business of America." *Labor Research Review* 1, no. 5 (1984): 129–32.

Fox, Robin. *Kinship and Marriage*. Baltimore, MD: Penguin Books, 1967.

"GDP—Gross Domestic Product." In *countryeconomy.com*. Accessed April 23, 2019. https://countryeconomy.com/gdp.

Geertz, Clifford. *The Interpretation of Cultures*. New York: Basic Book, 1973.

————. *Peddlers and Princes: Social Change and Economic Modernization in Two Indonesian Towns*. Chicago: University of Chicago Press, 1963.

Genocide. Frontline "The Triumph of Evil." Accessed May 26, 2019. file:///C:/Users/Bonzani%20Admin/Documents/Backup%20May%207%202017/Lexar/UK%20Classes/ANT%20101%20Introduction%20to%20Anthropology/The%20Crime%20Of%20Genocide%20_%20FRONTLINE%20_%20PBS.pdf.

Glenny, Misha. *The Fall of Yugoslavia: The Third Balkan War*. London: Penguin Books, 1992.

Goodenough, W. *Property, Kin, and Community on Truk*. New Haven: Yale University, 1951.

Gottlieb, Beatrice. *The Family in the Western World from the Black Death to the Industrial Age*. New York: Oxford University Press, 1993.

Grieder, William. *One World, Ready or Not: The Manic Logic of Global Capitalism*. New York: Simon and Schuster, 1997.

Harner, M. *The Jivaro, People of the Sacred Waterfalls* (A Doubleday Anchor book; AO-78). Garden City, NY: Anchor Press, Doubleday, 1973.

Hayden, Robert. "Serbian and Croatian Nationalism and the Wars in Yugoslavia." *Cultural Survival Quarterly* 19, no. 2 (1995): 25–28.

Heider, Karl G. *The Dugum Dani: A Papuan Culture in the Highlands of West New Guinea*. Viking Fund Publications in Anthropology Number Forty-Nine. New York: Wenner-Gren Foundation for Anthropological Research, 1970.

Heller, Joseph. *Catch-22*. New York: Simon & Schuster, 1961.

Hemming, John. *Red Gold: The Conquest of the Brazilian Indians*. London: Macmillan, 1978a.

————. *The Search for El Dorado*, 1st ed. New York: E. P. Dutton, 1978b.

————. *Amazon Frontier: The Defeat of the Brazilian Indians*. Cambridge, MA: Harvard University Press, 1987.

Herskovitz, Melville J. *Economic Anthropology: A Study in Comparative Economics*. New York: A. A. Knopf, 1952.

————. *The Economic Life of Primitive Peoples*. New York: A. A. Knopf, 1940.

Holldobler, Bert, and Edward O. Wilson. *The Ants*. Cambridge, MA: Harvard University Press, 1990.

International Covenant on Civil and Political Rights. Accessed June 12, 2019. //treaties.un.org/doc/publication/unts/volume%20999/volume-999-i-14668-english.pdf.

International Year of Cooperatives, United Nations. 2012. Accessed June 13, 2019. www.un.org/en/events/coopsyear/.

Human Relations Area Files, Yale University. Accessed June 18, 2019. www.hraf.yale.edu.

Janusek, John. "The Changing Face of Tiwanaku Residential Life: State and Local Identity in an Andean City." In *Tiwanaku and Its Hinterland: Archaeological and Paleoecological Investigations of an Andean Civilization*, vol. 11, edited by Alan L. Kolata. Washington, DC: Smithsonian Institution Press, 2002a.

————. "Out of Many, One: Style and Social Boundaries in Tiwanaku." *Latin American Antiquity* 13, no. 1 (2002b): 35–61.

Kolata, Alan L. *Tiwanaku and Its Hinterland: Archaeological and Paleoecological Investigations of an Andean Civilization*, vol. 11. Washington, DC: Smithsonian Institution Press, 2002.

————. *Tiwanaku: Portrait of an Andean Civilization*. Cambridge: Black well, 1993.

Kolata, Alan L., and Charles R. Ortloff. "Tiwanaku Raised-Field Agriculture in the Lake Titi caca Basin of Bolivia." In *Tiwanaku and Its Hinterland: Archaeology and Paleoecology of an Andean Civilization*, vol. 1, edited by Alan L. Kolata, 109–52. Washington, DC: Smithsonian Institution Press, 1996.

Kottak, Conrad Phillip. *Anthropology: Appreciating Human Diversity*, 15th ed. New York: McGraw-Hill, 2013.

Laland, K. N., F. J. Odling-Smee, and M. W. Feldman. "Evolutionary Consequences of Niche Construction and their Implications for Ecology." *Proceedings of the National Academy of Sciences USA* 96 (1999): 10242–0247.

Lee, Richard B. *The !Kung San: Men, Women and Work in a Foraging Society*. Cambridge: University Press, Cambridge and New York, 1979.

Lemarchand, René. "The Apocalypse in Rwanda." *Cultural Survival Quarterly* 18, no. 2 and 3 (1994): 29–33.

Lemkin, Raphael. *Axis Rule in Occupied Europe; Laws of Occupation, Analysis of Government, Proposals for Redress*. Washington: Carnegie Endowment for International Peace, Division of international law, 1944.

Lévi-Strauss, Claude. *The Elementary Structures of Kinship (Les Structures Elémentaires de la Parenté)*, revised ed. Translated from the French by James Harle Bell, John Richard von Sturmer, and edited by Rodney Needham. London: Eyre & Spottiswoode, 1969a.

———. *The Raw and the Cooked.* Translated from the French by John and Doreen Weightman. New York: Harper and Row, 1969b.

———. *Structural Anthropology.* New York: Basic Books, 1967.

———. *The Savage Mind (Pensée Sauvage).* Chicago, IL: University of Chicago Press, 1966.

———. *Tristes Tropiques: An Anthropological Study of Primitive Societies in Brazil.* Translated by John Russell. New York: Atheneum, 1964.

Malinowski, Bronislaw. *A Scientific Theory of Culture.* Chapel Hill, NC: The University of North Carolina Press, 1944.

———. *Argonauts of the Western Pacific: An Account of Native Enterprise and Adventure in the Archipelagoes of Melanesian New Guinea.* London: E.P. Dutton & Co., New York and G. Routledge & Sons, Ltd., 1922.

Mann, Charles. *1491: New Revelations of the Americas Before Columbus.* New York: Vintage Books, 2006.

"Martin Luther." In *History.* Accessed June 18, 2019. https://www.history.com/topics/reformation/martin-luther-and-the-95-theses.

Marx, Karl. *Capital.* Chicago: Charles H. Kerr and Co., 1867.

Marx, Karl, and Friedrich Engels. *Manifest der kommunistischen Partei.* London: The Communist League, 1848.

Mauss, Marcel. *The Gift: Forms and Functions of Exchange in Archaic Societies.* London: Cohen & West, Ltd., 1966 [1925].

Maybury-Lewis, David. *Indigenous Peoples, Ethnic Groups, and the State* (Cultural Studies in Ethnicity and Change), 2nd ed. Boston: Allyn and Bacon, 2002.

Meeks, Scott C., and David G. Anderson. "Drought, Subsistence Stress, and Population Dynamics: Assessing Mississippian Abandonment of the Vacant Quarter." In *Soils, Climate, and Society: Archaeological Investigations into Ancient America*, edited by John D. Wingard and Sue Eileen Hayes. Boulder: The University Press of Colorado, 2013, 61–84.

Mesoudi, A., A. Whiten, and K. N. Laland. "Towards a Unified Science of Cultural Evolution." *Behavioral and Brain Sciences* 29 (2006): 329–47.

———. Perspective: Is Human Cultural Evolution Darwinian? Evidence Reviewed from the Perspective of The Origin of Species. *Evolution* 58, no. 1 (2004): 1–11.

Mitades, Clanes Y. "Casas del Trapecio Amazónico Colombiano: Una Perspectiva Numerica de los Ticuna." *Amazonia em Cadernos,* no. 5 (2000): 39–68.

Moore, Jerry D. *A Prehistory of South America: Ancient Cultural Diversity on the Least Known Continent.* Boulder, CO: University Press of Colorado, 2014.

Morgan, Lewis Henry. *Ancient Society; or, Researches in the Lines of Human Progress from Savagery, through Barbarism to Civilization.* New York: H. Holt and Company, 1877.

———. *Systems of Consanguinity and Affinity of the Human Family.* Washington, DC: Smithsonian Institution, 1871.

———. *League of the Ho-dé-no-sau-nee or Iroquois.* Rochester: Sage & Brother Publishers, 1851.

———. "Introduction." In *League of the Iroquois. A Classic Study of an American Indian Tribe with the Original Illustrations*, edited by William N. Fenton. New Jersey: The Citadel Press, Secaucus, 1962 [1851].

Moseley, Michael E. *The Incas and Their Ancestors. The Archaeology of Peru,* revised ed. London: Thames & Hudson, 2001.

Murra, John Victor. "El 'control vertical' de un máximo de pisos ecológicos en la economía de las sociedades andinas." In *Visita de la Provincia de León de Huánuco en 1562, Tomo II,* edited by Iòigo Ortíz de Zuòiga. Lima: 1972, 429–68.

———. *The Economic Organization of the Inka State.* Greenwich, CT: JAI Press, 1980.

Nimuendajú, Curt. *The Tikuna.* Translated by W. D. Hohenthal and edited by Robert Lowie. Berkeley: University of California Publications in American Archaeology and Ethnology no. 45, 1952.

Nolan, Patrick, and Gerhard Lenski. *Human Societies: An Introduction to Macrosociology*, 10th ed. New York: McGraw Hill Publishers, 2006.

Odling-Smee, F. J., D. H. Erwin, E. P. Palkovacs, M. W. Feldman, and K. N. Laland. "Niche Construction Theory: A Practical Guide for Ecologists." *Quarterly Review of Biology* 88 (2013): 3–28.

Odling-Smee, F. J., K. N. Laland, and M. W. Feldman. *Niche Construction: The Neglected Process in Evolution.* Princeton, NJ: Princeton University Press, 2003.

Odling-Smee, J., and K. N. Laland. "Ecological Inheritance and Cultural Inheritance: What Are They and How Do They Differ?" *Biological Theory* 6 (2012): 220–30.

Oyuela-Caycedo, Augusto. "Dos Sitios Arqueológicos con Degrasante de Fibra Vegetal en la Serranía de San Jacinto (Departamento de Bolívar)." *Boletín de Arqueología* 2, no. 1 (1987): 5–26.

———. "Sedentism, Food Production, and Pottery Origins in the Tropics: San Jacinto 1; A Case Study in the Sabana de Bolivar, Serrania de San Jacinto, Colombia."

Unpublished PhD diss., Department of Anthropology, University of Pittsburgh, 1993.

————. "Rocks vs Clay: The Evolution of Pottery Technology in the Case of San Jacinto 1 (Colombia)." In *The Emergence of Pottery,* edited by William K. Barnett and John W. Hoopes, 133–44. Washington, DC: Smithsonian Institution Press, 1995.

————. "The Study of Collector Variability in the Transition to Sedentary Food Producers in Northern Colombia." *Journal of World Prehistory* 10, no. 1 (1996): 49–93.

————. "Seasonality in the Tropical Lowlands of Northwest South America: The Case of San Jacinto 1. Colombia." In *Seasonality and Sedentism,* edited by Thomas R. Rocek and Ofer Bar-Yosef, 165–79. Peabody Museum Bulletin 6, Cambridge: Harvard University, 1998.

————. What Can the AAA Do for Indigenous People in Colombia? *Anthropology News* 42, no. 7 (2001): 7.

————. "The Ecology of a Masked Dance: Negotiating at the Frontier of Identity in the Northwest Amazon." *Baessler-Archiv* 52 (2004): 54–74.

Oyuela-Caycedo, Augusto, and Juan José Vieco. La organización social de los Ticuna del Trapecio Amazonico Colombiano: Una aproximación cuantitativa. R*evista Colombiana de Antropología* 35 (1999): 146–79.

Oyuela-Caycedo, Augusto, and Manuela Fischer. "Ritual Paraphernalia and the Foundation of Religious Temples: The Case of the Tairona-Kágaba/Kogi, Sierra Nevada de Santa Marta, Colombia." *Baessler-Archiv* 54 (2006): 145–62.

Oyuela-Caycedo, Augusto, and Renée M. Bonzani. *San Jacinto 1: Ecologia Historica, Origenes de la Ceramica, e Inicios de la Vida Sedentaria en el Caribe Colombiano,* Spanish Editions. Barranquilla: Universidad del Norte, Colombia, 2014.

————. *San Jacinto 1: A Historical Ecological Approach to an Archaic Site in Colombia.* Tuscaloosa: University of Alabama Press, 2005.

Pálsson, Gísli. "Human-Environment Relations: Orientalism, Paternalism, and Communalism." In *Nature and Society, Anthropological Perspectives,* edited by Philippe Descola and Gísli Pálsson, 63–81. New York: Routledge, 1996.

Pauketat, Timothy R., and Thomas E. Emerson, eds. *Cahokia: Domination and Ideology in the Mississippian World.* Lincoln and London: University of Nebraska Press, 1997.

Platt, Tristan, Thérèse Bouysse-Cassagne, and Olivia Harris. Qaraqara-Charka. *Mallku, Inka y Rey en la provincia de Charcas (siglos XV-XVII): Historia antropológica de una confederación aymara.* Escocia. RU: University of St. Andrews, 2006.

Polanyi, Karl. *The Great Transformation.* New York: Farrar & Rinehart, Inc., 1944.

Politis, Gustavo G. "Moving to Produce: Nukak Mobility and Settlement Patterns in Amazonia." *World Archaeology* 27, no. 3 (1996): 492–511.

Pool, Chris. *Olmec Archaeology and Early Mesoamerica.* Cambridge: Cambridge University Press, 2007.

Pool, Christopher A. *Olmec Archaeology and Early Mesoamerica.* Cambridge: Cambridge University Press, 2007.

Price, T. Douglas, and Gary M. Feinman. *Images of the Past,* 5th ed. New York: McGraw-Hill, 2008.

Price, T. Douglas, and James H. Burton. *An Introduction to Archaeological Chemistry.* New York: Springer, 2011.

Radcliffe-Brown, Alfred Reginald. *Structure and Function in Primitive Societies.* Glencoe, IL: Free Press, 1952.

————. *The Andaman Islanders.* England: Cambridge University Press, 1933.

Reichel-Dolmatoff, Gerardo. *Rainforest Shamans.* Devon: Themis Books, 1997.

————. "Cosmology as Ecological Analysis: A View from the Rain Forest." *Man* 11, no. 3 (1976): 307–18.

Resek, Carl. *Lewis Henry Morgan: American Scholar.* Chicago, IL: The University of Chicago Press, 1960.

Rousseau, Jean-Jacques. *The Social Contract.* New York: Penguin Books, 1987 [1762].

Sahlins, Marshall David. *Stone Age Economics.* Chicago: Aldine-Atherton, 1972.

————. "Notes on the Original Affluent Society." In *Man the Hunter,* edited by R.B. Lee and I. DeVore, 85–89. New York: Aldine Publishing Company, 1968.

Santos Granero, Fernando. "Power, Ideology and the Ritual of Production in Lowland South America." *Royal Anthropological Institute of Great Britain and Ireland* 21, no. 4 (1986): 657–79.

Schneider, David, and Kathleen Gough, eds. *Matrilineal Kinship.* Berkeley: University of California Press, 1961.

Sharer, Robert J. *The Ancient Maya,* 5th ed. Stanford, CA: Stanford University Press, 1994.

Shimada, Izumi, Crystal Baker Schaaf, Lonnie G. Thompson, and Ellen Mosley-Thompson. "Cultural Impacts of Severe Droughts in the Prehistoric Andes: Application of 1500-Year Ice Core Precipitation Record." *World Archaeology* 22, no. 3 (1991): 247–70.

"Sibling." In *Online Etymology Dictionary.* Accessed June 8, 2019. https://www.etymonline.com/word/sibling.

Smith, Adam. *An Inquiry into the Nature and Causes of the Wealth of Nations.* London: W. Strahan and T. Cadell, 1776.

Smith, B. D. "A Cultural Niche Construction Theory of Initial Domestication." *Biological Theory* 6 (2012): 260–71.

———. "Niche Construction and the Behavioral Context of Plant and Animal Domestication." *Evolutionary Anthropology: Issues, News, and Reviews* 16 (2007a): 188–99.

———. "The Ultimate Ecosystem Engineers." *Science* 315 (2007b): 1797–798.

Smith, C. J. *The Roman Clan: The Gens from Ancient Ideology to Modern Anthropology.* Cambridge, UK: Cambridge University Press, 2006.

Spencer, Herbert. *First Principles.* New York: D. Appleton, 1886.

Steward, Julian H. *Theory of Culture Change: The Methodology of Multilinear Evolution*. Urbana: University of Illinois Press, 1955.

Stockard, Janice E. *Marriage in Culture. Practice and Meaning across Diverse Societies.* Belmont, CA: Wadsworth, 2002.

"The Crime of Genocide." In *Frontline.* Accessed June 18, 2019. https://www.pbs.org/wgbh/pages/frontline/shows/rwanda/reports/dsetexhe.html.

The Detroit News. "FCA reconsiders plan to move all Ram production to Mich." October 29, 2018. https://www.detroitnews.com/story/business/autos/chrysler/2018/10/29/fca-reconsiders-plan-move-all-ram-production-warren-michigan/1809407002/.

The Universal Declaration of Human Rights, United Nations. Accessed June 12, 2019. www.un.org/en/universal-declaration-human-rights/.

"Two Lancashire Looms." In *Wikipedia.* Accessed April 24, 2019. https://en.wikipedia.org/wiki/File:QSMM_Two_Lancashire_looms.ogv.

Tykot, Robert H., and Tamsey K. Andrews. *Sardinia in the Mediterranean—A Footprint in the Sea: Studies in Sardinian Archaeology Presented to Miriam S. Balmuth,* Monographs in Mediterranean Archaeology 3. Sheffield: Sheffield Academic Press, 1992.

Tylor, Edward Burnett. *Primitive Culture.* London: John Murray, 1871.

United States Declaration of Independence. Accessed May 8, 2019. http://archives.gov/exhibits/charters/declaration_transcript.html.

USA Today Special Report. Record Refugee Flights Hit All Parts of the Globe. November 20–22, 2015.

Van Gennep, Arnold. *The Rites of Passage.* London: Routledge, 2004 [1908].

Veblen, Thorstein. *The Theory of the Leisure Class.* New York: Macmillan, 1899.

Ward, Martha. *Nest in the Wind: Adventures in Anthropology in a Tropical Island,* 2nd ed. Long Grove, IL: Waveland Press, Inc., 2005.

Weber, Max. *Agrarian Sociology of Ancient Civilization.* London: NLB; Atlantic Highlands, NJ: Humanities Press, 1976 [1897, 1889, 1909].

———. *Economy and Society.* Translated by E. Fischoff et al. New York: Bedminster Press, 1968 [1922].

———. *The Sociology of Religion.* Boston: Beacon Press, 1963 [1922].

———. *The Protestant Ethic and the Spirit of Capitalism.* G. London: Allen & Unwin, Ltd., 1930 [1904–5, 1920].

White, Leslie. *The Evolution of Culture.* Left Coast Press, CA: Walnut Creek, 2007 [1959].

———. *The Science of Culture: A Study of Man and civilization.* New York: Farrar, Straus and Giroux, 1969 [1949].

Wiessner, Polly. "Risk, Reciprocity and Social Influences on !Kung San Economics." In *Politics and History in Band Societies,* edited by Eleanor Leacock and Richard Lee, 61–84. New York: Cambridge University Press, 1982.

Woodard, Colin. *American Nations: A History of the Eleven Rival Regional Cultures of North America*. New York: Viking, 2011.

World Population, United States Census Bureau. Accessed June 12, 2019. www.census.gov/popclock/.

Zeder, M. A. "The Broad Spectrum Revolution at 40: Resource Diversity, Intensification, and an Alternative to Optimal Foraging Explanations." *Journal of Anthropological Archaeology* 31 (2012): 241–64.

Index